W9-ABY-018

ND 497 .T8 N4

Museum of Modern Art (New
  York, N.Y.)

Turner

TURNER : IMAGINATION AND REALITY

The Burning of the Houses of Parliament. 1835. Oil on canvas, 36½ × 48½″. The Cleveland Museum of Art (John L. Severance Collection)

Turner: Imagination and Reality

Lawrence Gowing

THE MUSEUM OF MODERN ART, NEW YORK

Distributed by Doubleday & Company, Inc, Garden City, New York

TRUSTEES OF THE MUSEUM OF MODERN ART

David Rockefeller, Chairman of the Board; Henry Allen Moe, William S. Paley, Vice-Chairmen; Mrs Bliss Parkinson, President; James Thrall Soby, Ralph F. Colin, Gardner Cowles, Vice-Presidents; Willard C. Butcher, Treasurer; Walter Bareiss, Alfred H. Barr, Jr, *Mrs Robert Woods Bliss, William A. M. Burden, Ivan Chermayeff, *Mrs W. Murray Crane, John de Menil, René d'Harnoncourt, Mrs C. Douglas Dillon, Mrs Edsel B. Ford, *Mrs Simon Guggenheim, Wallace K. Harrison, Mrs Walter Hochschild, *James W. Husted, Philip Johnson, Mrs Albert D. Lasker, John L. Loeb, *Ranald H. Macdonald, Porter A. McCray, *Mrs G. Macculloch Miller, Mrs Charles S. Payson, *Duncan Phillips, Mrs John D. Rockefeller 3rd, Nelson A. Rockefeller, Mrs Wolfgang Schoenborn, Mrs Bertram Smith, Mrs Donald B. Straus, *Edward M. M. Warburg, *Monroe Wheeler, John Hay Whitney

*Honorary Trustee

1966, All Rights Reserved
The Museum of Modern Art
11 West 53 Street, New York, N.Y. 10019
Library of Congress Catalogue Card No. 66–16676
Printed in Great Britain by Balding + Mansell,
London and Wisbech
Designed by Brian N. Rushton

FOREWORD AND ACKNOWLEDGEMENTS

Self-evidently The Museum of Modern Art has always dedicated itself to the exhibition and general understanding of contemporary art, but from time to time it includes in its programme exceptional productions of other periods of art history in which the modern spirit happened to be fore-shadowed or by which modern artists have been influenced. We have no precedent for a one-man show of an artist who died more than a century ago.

Proclaimed a painter by his father when he was fourteen, a full member of the Royal Academy at twenty-four, Turner became the most successful practitioner of landscape painting in England. In his forties, proud and rich and idio-syncratic, he found himself revolutionizing his art, eliminating from it linear draughtsmanship and classical composition; glorifying only light and shade, by the sole means of colour. Transcending the concepts of romantic art, he reached out into the borderland between representation and the abstract.

These modern aspects of Turner's art with which this exhibition is particularly concerned scarcely appear in the work exhibited in his lifetime. He left to the nation approximately three hundred oils and nineteen thousand watercolours and drawings. For the most part, the most revolutionary pictures were not placed on exhibition until the present century, and some of the watercolours exhibited here have not previously been shown even in England.

Influences in art are always obscure and arguable. Just as a single bird may drop a seed upon an island and thereby alter its entire vegetation and animal ecology, a mere engraving or newspaper clipping, chancing to catch the eye of an individual painter, may change the direction of his lifework, and he may not even know it. The French impressionists and their analysts and critics have, almost to a man, denied Turner's influence, and yet relationship of some sort is strikingly apparent. In all history, including art history, a kind of prophecy is inherent and unexplainable. Something in the spirit of the age, the affinities and rivalries of nations, and inter-weavings of one art with another, motivate individual artists of various schools, all at the same time, in the way of an unconscious response to the cultural matrix. Presumably none of the present-day abstract painters whose

principal means of expression is light and colour had Turner and his life-work in mind; but looking back upon their revolution, more than a hundred years later than his, we see a kinship.

The exhibition which this catalogue records has been made possible by the generosity of The National Gallery, The Tate Gallery and The British Museum. We have added to their contributions a half-dozen masterworks from American collections. The planning of it began several years ago, when The Honourable William A. M. Burden was President of the Museum, and he has given it his distinguished personal attention throughout.

The Trustees of The Museum of Modern Art are no less beholden to His Excellency Sir Patrick Dean, British Ambassador to the United States, and to the Chairmen of the Trustees and Directors of the British national collections: Sir Colin Anderson and Mr Norman Reid of The Tate Gallery; The Right Honourable Viscount Radcliffe and Sir Frank Francis of the British Museum; and The Right Honourable Lord Robbins and Sir Philip Hendy of The National Gallery.

On behalf of the Trustees of The Museum of Modern Art, I also warmly acknowledge the scholarship and devoted endeavour of my co-director of the exhibition, Mr Lawrence Gowing, Keeper of British Painting at The Tate Gallery. Mr Martin Butlin has allowed us to call on his wide knowledge, and others at The Tate Gallery who have been especially helpful are Miss Judith Cloake, Mr Stefan Slabczynski, Mr Leslie Parris, and Mr Brian N. Rushton, who has seen this catalogue through the press. At the British Museum, Mr Edward Croft-Murray, Mr Paul Hulton and Mr Reginald Williams, and at The National Gallery, Sir Philip Hendy and Mr Martin Davies have been equally courteous and efficacious in our behalf.

Particular thanks are also due to the Trustees of the collaborating American museums and their Directors: Mr Sherman E. Lee, of The Cleveland Museum of Art, Mr Perry T. Rathbone, of the Boston Museum of Fine Arts, Mr John Maxon, of The Art Institute of Chicago, Mr Evan Turner, of the Philadelphia Museum of Art, Mr Otto Wittmann, of The Toledo Museum of Art and Mr Wilbur D. Peat, of the Herron Museum of Art, and to Mrs Flora Whitney Miller, of New York. For special support I am indebted to Mrs Vincent Astor, Mrs McCauley Conner, Mrs John Barry Ryan, Mrs Arnold Whitridge and Mr Gardner Cowles. We owe much to the help of Mr John Gage and Mr Michael Kitson, who have placed the results of their researches at our disposal. Deep thanks and appreciation are also extended to Sir Kenneth Clark, Sir John Rothenstein, Mr William C. Seitz, Mr Adrian Stokes, Mr John Russell, Mr Harold Joachim, Miss Frances Keech, Miss Jane Rye and Miss Françoise Boas.

MONROE WHEELER
Director of Exhibitions and Publications
The Museum of Modern Art, New York

Buttermere Lake. 1797–8. Oil, 35 × 47". The Tate Gallery, London

There is a special reason for looking at Turner. We are aware that in his painting something singular and incomparable happened. It astounded and bewildered his contemporaries and it is still not altogether comprehensible today. In the pictures that Turner showed — and concealed — in the last two decades of his life a change was evidently taking place of a kind that is disturbing to an artist's public. The critic who wrote in 1839 of imagination and reality striving for mastery in Turner's works was in no doubt that reality was suffering a lamentable defeat. It is evident that both the kind of reality and the order of imagination that painting had traditionally offered were changing in Turner's hands. Since his time such transformations have recurred with increasing frequency. We are now familiar with the disturbance that they make. We are far from familiar with Turner.

We cannot show the whole of Turner. It is not certain that we are yet prepared to see him whole. The aim of the present exhibition is to take a close and concentrated look at one side of his achievement, the development that is characteristic of the last twenty years of his career. Of course, one cannot separate an artist's late works from the rest; his meaning unfolds throughout his life. To understand the direction of Turner's development, it is necessary to look first at his starting point and at some of the studies and drawings of subsequent years that prepared the way for his ultimate achievement.

In Turner's first pictures imagination and reality seem like opposite alternatives. *Buttermere Lake*, which he exhibited when he was twenty-three, is real. We are hardly aware of the picturesque arrangement of the scene. The banks of shadow have the gentle breadth of tone that Turner had learned copying watercolours by J. R. Cozens, in the company of Girtin, but the picture seems almost styleless. To a contemporary it looked merely dull. Hoppner, the fashionable portraitist, went to Turner's studio to see it and pronounced him 'a timid man afraid to venture'. To us the stillness has a different meaning. It gives a sense of awe, as if the painter and subject were both subdued by the unearthly majesty of light.

Turner's vision of the rainbow over Buttermere was poetic, and he knew it. It was one of the pictures to which he attached lines of poetry in the Academy catalogue, for the first time. For *Buttermere* he strung together fragments of Thomson's *Spring*, as if forcing them to compose a poem of his own. Significantly, he avoided the lines in which 'the showery prism' unfolded the colours of Newton's spectrum. His poem was different, and colour still had little part in it. Light and the grandeur that it gave the place excluded everything else. But as the light fell it scattered shining flecks, sprinklings of incandescent pigment. They suggest that one other thing was as real to him, the paint itself.

Turner soon corrected the impression of timidity. *The Fifth Plague of Egypt*, exhibited two years later, is a grand imaginative invention (p. 8). Yet its origin was similar. Impressions of a storm in the mountains of North Wales were grafted onto the style of Poussin to make a formidable

George Dance: *Portrait of Turner*. March 31st, 1800. Pencil, 10 × 7¾". The Royal Academy, London*

The fifth plague of Egypt. 1800. Oil, 49 × 72″. Art Association of Indianapolis, Herron Museum of Art

manifestation of the Sublime — the representation, in Burke's words, of 'whatever is in any sort terrible'. Turner's natural sense of awe had become linked with his ambition and his sense of style. We do not think of sheer ambition as a particularly creative or sympathetic quality in an artist, but in Turner it was surely both. He wrote in one of his sketchbooks an invocation:

O Heaven avert the impending care,
O make my future prospects fair.

The Fifth Plague, which actually represented the Seventh, for Turner had no particular interest in any part of the Bible but the Apocalypse, was the first of his great gestures of emulation. The equation of the weather of North Wales with the thunder and hail and the fire that ran along the ground was the beginning of a long engrossment in the force of nature. In the years that followed, Turner was, in fact, compiling a collection both of overwhelming natural effects and of compelling artistic styles. The hostile power of nature provided a series of subjects that culminated in *Hannibal Crossing the Alps*, in which the giant stride of a storm across a Yorkshire moor inspired a picture as styleless and original as *Buttermere*. But he gave an equal force to his other theme, the pictures of fair prospects. In combination the two were irresistible. Light and the elements were not only Turner's subjects; they were his as allies in carrying everything before him. He was never again accused of timidity and in a year or two we hear that Hoppner 'reprobated the presumptive manner in which he paints.'

Turner's presumption was certainly enormous. The historic styles were engrossing painters everywhere, but the vigour and resource with which he seized on them were quite exceptional. He took the past by storm, and his pictures were soon being 'compared . . . and rather preferred to the greatest masters'. But the extravagance of what followed placed him beyond the pale of tradition. In 1801 a critic already detected in the first of his sea-pieces in the Dutch manner an affectation of carelessness. Sir George Beaumont, the magisterial connoisseur, pronounced against him. 'Turner', he said, 'is perpetually aiming to be extraordinary, but rather produces works that are capricious and singular than great.'

Beaumont became the leader of the opposition to Turner, and the diarist Farington, who wrote down everyone's opinion in the hope of developing his own, recorded the hostile judgments year by year. Turner painted 'strong skies and parts not corresponding to them'; he made nothing out; he had no power of execution; his foregrounds were 'comparative blots'. The word is interesting, and it recurs in the comments. Turner's figures, someone said, were 'left like blots'. Fuseli told Northcote that the *Holy Family* was 'like the embryo or blot of a great master of colouring'. Alexander Cozens's 'new method' of generating landscapes from random blots was common knowledge. Turner's effects look to us far from haphazard. But to his contemporaries they evidently recalled the tradition of random suggestion that goes back to Leonardo and his famous

Snow Storm: Hannibal Crossing the Alps. 1812.
Oil on canvas, 57 × 93″. The Tate Gallery, London*

9

Calais Pier. 1803.
Oil on canvas, 67¾ × 94½″. The Tate Gallery, London*
A detail is reproduced above

recommendation to assist invention by looking at the stains on old walls or the veins of stones. Indeed, Hoppner told Farington that Turner 'left so much to be imagined that it was like looking into a coal fire or upon an old wall'. Beaumont said that the water in *Calais Pier* was 'like the veins in a marble slab'.

It was clear that the consistency of representation had altered; the intention had shifted. The purpose was no longer to deploy an accepted vocabulary of representation. Water, for example, was expected to be sea-green and transparent. Turner was careless of the convention. He required a ruder and more real substance, which appeared outrageously incongruous. In 1802 his waves were said to be chalky; in 1803 his sea looked like soap and chalk; in 1804 the water in his picture reminded Opie of a turnpike road over the sea and in 1805 Benjamin West said it was like stone.

It was not only a conventional code of figuration that was breaking down under Turner's relentless pressure. The whole condition of painting was in question. It had been founded on an axiom derived from classical sources, the axiom, as Fuseli put it, 'that the less the traces appear of the means by which a work has been produced, the more it resembles the operations of nature'. The traces of Turner's means were unconcealed. In 1805 he was applying paint freely and visibly with the palette knife. Wilkie, who had just arrived in London with an admiration for Teniers, thought it the most abominable workmanship he ever saw; only the effect was natural. By the next year there was a host of young painters working in the new manner. 'It is the scribbling of painting,' a critic remarked, 'so much of the trowel — so mortary.' Painting was now required to resemble itself before anything else; the operations portrayed were first and foremost the painter's. The change was a lasting one and twenty years later a writer described what had happened. 'It is evident that Mr Constable's landscapes are like nature; it is still more evident that they are like paint.' It is the fact that this became the new condition of painting that makes the old criticisms now read like praise.

Turner imparted his personal force to whatever he touched, and he touched almost everything. It was equally evident whether he was painting in the idyllic convention of Claude or in the ferocious manner which he grafted on to the Dutch sea-piece. Hazlitt called his pictures 'a waste of morbid strength'. 'They give pleasure,' he wrote, 'only by the excess of power triumphing over the barrenness of the subject'. Turner's pictures indeed became increasingly barren of the kind of substance that had furnished traditional landscape. The descriptive detail and the reticent skills of his prototypes were assumed or neglected. He was intent on the scheme and the effect of a picture, and intent on outdoing whichever master it had come from. The pictorial idea was imaginatively recreated, with a summary force that seemed to put the original in the shade. It was reasonable that connoisseurs should be outraged. Turner's attitude betrayed an egotism and an insensitivity to the virtue of classical self-effacement which were as formidable as his talent.

Turner isolated the pictorial effect, as one skims the cream off milk. He proceeded to synthesize it afresh with an almost excessive richness. To complete the product he was apt to add synthetic details; we do not always find them convincing. His essential creation did not require them, and eventually he realized it. He had isolated an intrinsic quality of painting and revealed that it could be self-sufficient, an independent imaginative function. His imagination was like an insatiable appetite. Every type and effect of painting seemed equally at his disposal. He treated them as if they were incidental to a common property inherent in all of them — the property of serving some exorbitant requirement of his own, which the whole of art and of nature together could hardly have satisfied. At the opening of the Academy in 1806 Farington met two critics looking at a Turner. One of them said, 'That is madness.' The other agreed: 'He is a madman.'

Coast Scene near Naples, 1828?
Oil, 16 × 23¾″. The Tate Gallery, London

We can follow the process in the story of Turner's relation to Claude, the example that meant most to him and occupied him longest. At the age of twenty-four he told Farington how a great picture, one of the Altieri Claudes, had struck him: 'He was both pleased and unhappy while he viewed it, it seemed to be beyond the power of imitation.' The challenge became a crucial one. When Turner became Professor of Perspective at the Academy, he described Claude's achievement to his students:

> The golden orient or the amber-coloured ether, the midday ethereal vault and fleecy skies, resplendent valleys . . . rich, harmonious, true and clear, replete with all the aerial qualities of distance, aerial lights, aerial colour. . .

There remained a conflict. In one draft of the lecture he wrote that 'all of the valuable freshness and beauties' only tempted the spectator 'to deny that nature never did or could appear so artificially deceitful'. The tortuous syntax is revealing; eventually the sentence was deleted altogether. It would have been imprudent to accuse Claude of artifice and duplicity. The classical taste was a veritable tyranny.

Landscape with Water. c. 1840–5.
Oil, 48 × 71¾″. The Tate Gallery, London

Anyone who brought to painting a force and an ambition like Turner's found himself in rivalry with the past. Beaumont and his colleagues were known to be determined 'to deprive the first genius of the day of encouragement and set up inferior works to put him down'. When Turner bequeathed two of his pictures, one in the Claudian manner, the other in the Dutch, to hang beside a Claude in the National Gallery, it was intended as the final settling of scores.

Turner, in fact, took both sides. The stillness and the exact gradations of radiant light always formed one aspect of his art — 'pure as Italian air, calm, beautiful and serene,' as he described Claude. Continually complementing it was the opposite aspect, the turbulent journey through storm and catastrophe. Turner beat the classical taste with Claude's own weapons. He not only borrowed the style, and turned

San Giorgio from the Dogana, Venice: Sunrise. 1819. Watercolour, 8 ⅛ × 11 ⅛″. The British Museum, London

the enemy flank with it; he made a profound study of Claude's method. 'Where', he asked himself in his lecture on landscape, 'through all these comprehensive qualities and powers, can we find a clue towards his mode of practice?'

> We must consider how he could have attained such powers but by continual study of parts of nature. Parts, for, had he not so studied, we should have found him sooner pleased with simple subjects of nature, and would not have as we now have, pictures made up of bits, but pictures of bits.

Claude, in fact, demonstrated to Turner, perhaps the more vividly because of a certain literalness that they shared, something about the imaginative synthesis of art and the way that it transforms reality. The direct visual transcriptions, which were to be characteristic of the nineteenth century, seemed to Turner merely pictures of bits. The epitaph which he wrote on the new style before it was fairly born is hard to improve on. Visual realism was *pleased with simple subjects*. Turner, generally speaking, was not, and the character of his art was due to the fact.

Turner rarely painted pictures of bits. In the first decade of the century, when modern *plein-airisme* was beginning, he made a series of oil-sketches with a delightful grace and fluency. Twenty years later in Italy he painted, among other subjects, *A Hill Town on the Edge of a Plain*, surely from nature (p. 59). The sketch was his nearest and his last approach to the emerging lyrical realism of the time.

Apart from this, Turner hardly ever painted from nature. He once exclaimed to an artist who had been searching vainly for an old motive, 'What, do you not know yet, at your age, that you ought to paint your impressions?' His sense of the word was exactly opposite to the one that has been sanctified by later usage. He painted the kind of impressions that remained in the memory for years or decades. Ruskin pointed out that Turner seemed 'either never to have lost, or cared to disturb, the impression made on him by any scene'. His compositions were, in Ruskin's words, 'perhaps universally an arrangement of remembrance'.

No painter has made a more continual study of parts of nature than Turner. At his death his studio still contained more than 19,000 drawings. But it was not only his unremitting industry that was remarkable. The significant thing was his awareness of his standpoint. In the heyday of the Romantic engrossment in nature, he had no doubt that art was founded on art. In 1809 he was one of the subscribers to Opie's *Lectures on Painting* and a note he made in the margin of the book gives a clear description of his method. Opie warned the student to study art as well as nature, 'not contenting himself with a superficial survey, but studying attentively the peculiar manner of each master'. It was the implication that there was any other possibility that aroused, as Turner said, his gall:

> He that has that ruling enthusiasm which accompanies abilities cannot look superficially. Every glance is a glance for study: contemplating and defining qualities and causes, effects and incidents, and develops by practice the possibility of attaining what appears mysterious upon principle. Every look at nature is a refinement upon art. Each tree and blade of grass or flower is not to him the individual tree, grass or flower, but what it is in relation to the whole, its tone, its contrast and its use, and how far practicable: admiring Nature by the power and practicability of his Art, and judging of his Art by the perceptions drawn from Nature.

It is characteristic of Turner that there is no suggestion that art is at the service of nature. On the contrary, the look at nature is inspired by art and made entirely with reference to it. For Turner artistic perception was primarily a modification of expectations, and a slight one, for his expectations amounted to imperious demands. It is curious that his account of representation should be nearer to the account offered by the psychology of perception than to any aesthetic view between his day and ours. His turn of mind was practical and sceptical; an acute observer, the future Lady Eastlake, who met him in old age, called him 'a cynical kind of body, who seems to love his art for no other reason than because it is his own'. He knew by instinct where the reality of painting lay.

The nature of Turner's originality was already clear to his contemporaries, clearer in some ways than it is now. In 1816 Hazlitt wrote an essay on what he called pedantry and affectation in the arts:

> We here allude particularly to Turner, the ablest landscape-painter now living, whose pictures are however, too much abstractions of aerial perspective, and representations not properly of the objects of nature as of the medium through which they were seen. They are the triumph of the knowledge of the artist and of the power of the pencil over the barrenness of the subject. They are pictures of the elements of air, earth and water. The artist delights to go back to the first chaos of the world, or to that state of things, when the waters were separated from the dry land, and light from darkness, but as yet no living thing nor tree bearing fruit was seen on the face of the earth. All is without form and void. Someone said of his landscapes that they were *pictures of nothing and very like*.

The qualities which we know in the painting of Turner's sixties were sufficiently apparent twenty years earlier to make a good critic angry, and his anger yields a glimpse of the truth. Only the final remark seems at first reading unperceptive. Turner's work is never without a figurative reference. Yet the remark is the kind of abuse, so familiar in the history of modern art, that sticks and provides a useful label for something that defies description. In the decades after Hazlitt wrote, Turner's vision grew steadily broader and less specific. It offers, perhaps, pictures of everything rather than of nothing. But eventually no single touch of paint corresponded to any specific object; the equivalence

The Burning of the Houses of Parliament. 1834. Watercolour from a sketchbook. 9¼ × 12¾″. The British Museum, London

Buildings by a Lake. Watercolour and Pencil. 1845. 9⅛ × 12¾″. The British Museum, London

was between the whole configuration and the total subject. Moreover, the transformation that it achieved — and this was Hazlitt's strangest and most convincing insight —seems to us like the return to a primal flux which denies the separate identity of things.

The early critics of Turner were goaded to the point at which they almost realized that painting was uncovering, not only new means of representation, but a new substance, a different order of reality. What Hazlitt detected in 1816 was the alarming imminence of a kind of painting that was irreconcilable with the classical tradition. Twenty years later this new kind of painting was fully formed. Feeling his way towards it, Turner was guided by experience of the relatively informal medium that he used in topographical draughtsmanship, his original trade. Watercolour demonstrated the possibility of a tonal consistency both lighter and cooler than that of the classical convention. Sir George Beaumont said, in his judicial way, that 'much harm had been done by endeavouring to make painting in oil appear like watercolours, by which, in endeavouring to give lightness and clearness, the force of oil painting has been lost.' When Beaumont's opposition made oil pictures difficult to sell, Turner fell back on watercolour and the mass market for engravings of his drawings. He was as secure as the *rentier* painters of succeeding generations in France. Opposition left him unaffected. Indeed it confirmed him in his defiant independence. His practice provided him, alone among Romantic artists, with a continual supply of new motives, and a field in which the rule of the grand manner was largely relaxed. A medium in which the effects come half by chance requires confidence in the element in painting that is involuntary and unrehearsed, a confidence that Turner was very ready to develop. He was inclined from the beginning toward an empirical, extempore approach. As a young man he had spoken of it to Farington — indeed he mentioned it twice, and one can imagine the truculence in his tone: 'Turner has no settled process but drives the colours about till he has expressed the idea in his mind.'

Turner's probing, experimental use of watercolour was unique in painting before Cézanne. He used the medium constantly throughout his life; his work in it was always a step ahead of that in oil. Watercolour never served him better than on his first journey to Italy in 1819. He had been painting Italy for nearly twenty years; or rather, he had been painting Italian painting, recreating and refining the classical landscape convention. He went to Italy in search of the material of specific pictorial effects. The notes in his sketchbooks record his eagerness, which was rewarded when he reached Loreto and he was able to write, 'The first bit of Claude'. It was, however, at Venice in the drawings which he made at dawn that what Hazlitt called his abstractions of aerial perspective culminated (p. 12). A few months after his essay Hazlitt had written a review that made his criticism more specific. He explained that Turner's colours were 'not local colours with an atmosphere passing over them, but' (the habit of abuse returning) 'a combination of

Venice, Looking East from the Giudecca at Sunrise. 1819.
Watercolour, 8 ⅞ × 11 ⅞".
The British Museum, London

Sunset, Returning from Torcello. 1835? Watercolour, 9½ × 11⅞". The British Museum, London

Ehrenbreitstein. c. 1842–4. Watercolour and pen, 9¾ × 11 ⅛″. The British Museum, London

gaudy hues intended to become a striking point of attraction on the walls of the exhibition'. Turner had always resisted local colour. His notes on the old masters were largely devoted to demonstrating to himself that it was sublimity and naturalness that 'a creative mind must be imprest by', not 'historic colour' (whether full and strong in the Roman manner or corrupted by mixing and breaking in the Bolognian style, as Reynolds had classified them). His criticism of the figures in Poussin's *Deluge* is revealing: '... they are positively red, blue and yellow, while the sick and wan sun is not allowed to shed one ray but tears.' The worst that he could say of an artist was, as he said of Rubens, that he 'could not be happy with the bare simplicity of pastoral scenery or the immutable laws of nature's light and shade'.

In the pictures that Hazlitt was thinking of, the colours of distance were already so purged of local admixtures that they appeared schematic. Three years later, when he arrived in Venice, Turner went farther. It may have been due to the light, but he was perhaps as much affected by the spirit of the place, which Fuseli, whose teaching was often in his mind, called 'the birthplace and the theatre of colour'. In his drawings done at daybreak the scene is made of colour, with no other substance. Shape is outlined with a marvellous economy of touch, as if discovering itself of its own accord. The colour lies intact and pearly on the paper.

These drawings leave a magical impression that the specific details of a real place grew out of colour instead of the reverse. There is good evidence that this is what actually happened in at least some of the drawings of this kind. In the Venice and Como sketchbook, from which these drawings come, the finished subjects are followed by three pages that bear only parallel zones of colour, painted horizontally across the sheet. They are evidently the beginnings of future drawings, and at the same time experiments in the property that these combinations of pure colour possess of creating a light and a reality of their own. One can imagine in the bands of colour the material of earth and sky, stone and water, incandescent in cool morning light. Probably they were allowed to suggest their own purpose, and left waiting until the moment for it arose. The colour beginnings in the Venice and Como book are the earliest that survive. Their radiance is pale and watery by comparison with the richness of later examples. But other drawings from the journey confirm what was happening in Turner's art. The old hierarchy of reality was reversed. Colour assumed precedence. It existed first and provided the imaginative substance out of which the likeness of an external subject could be made.

The watercolours of Venice are delicate and objective. But so far from inaugurating Impressionism, they were very nearly the end of it in Turner's work. Once the atmospheric gradations of Claude had been followed to their source, they hardly occupied him for their own sake again. The Venetian watercolours may well have been made from nature. Turner is known to have used watercolour in front of a subject again, fifteen years later, on an equally crucial occasion. But his usual practice was different. It was described in 1819 in a letter from the spendthrift son of Soane, the architect, to his father:

> Turner is in the neighbourhood of Naples making rough pencil sketches to the astonishment of the Fashionables, who wonder what use these rough draughts can be — simple souls! At Rome a sucking blade of the brush made the request of going out with pig Turner to colour — he grunted for answer that it would take up too much time to colour in the open air — he could make 15 or 16 pencil sketches to one coloured, and then grunted his way home.

During the day, on his sketching tours, he drew in pencil. His drawings were already considered rough in 1819. In the decades that followed the intrinsic quality of the medium asserted itself more and more in this field too, and avalanches of separate pencil marks fall across pages of Turner's sketchbooks, making not contours but a scattered drift of lines in which objects could be distinguished or lost at will. Drawing provided the framework on which the colours that he carried in his head could be hung later. The watercolours were made in his lodgings at night. His memory was phenomenal, yet this was not entirely a feat of memory. In the *Monte Gennaro* of 1819 Turner was already very evidently recording not so much an impression of a scene as a potentiality of paint (p. 28). In the later watercolours there is no sense that an actual tone or hue was precisely observed and recollected. It seems rather that the experience of a place and the day-time engrossment in topography allowed Turner to meditate on some unexplored property of his vast technical resources, some possibility inherent in colour and in paint itself. In the *Ehrenbreitstein*, painted more than twenty years later, three bands of colour lie across the paper. At the top there is a delicate iridescence as of sky, at the bottom watery yellow-brown broken with blue, like the reflecting surface of a river, and between them, broader than either, a band of pink. The way that this pink is fretted, rubbed and dappled with rock-brown, smoke-grey, mist-blue and yellow like evening sunlight is the subject of the picture. It is the paint, or rather the whole technical repertory and its capacity of metaphoric evocation, as much as the picturesque subject, that are real to us. In art and in nature Turner was concerned with a similar, related property. It was the property in each which, to judge from his marginal note to Opie, he seems, in his practical way, to have called *practicability*. The significant word recurs in his lectures; he was impatient of anything else, and sometimes he seems hardly to have distinguished any other property in things around him. He was concerned with the capacity of paint and nature together to fulfil an imperative requirement of his own.

The experience of Italy had a profound effect on Turner. His steady production of exhibition-pictures was interrupted. Much of his energy went for a time into watercolours. They were not only easier to sell; they reflected much better the 'bland but luminous communion of light',

Rough Sea with Wreckage. c. 1830. Oil on canvas, 36 × 48¼″. The Tate Gallery, London

of which a critic wrote in 1822. His experience of art in Italy inspired a vast and uneasy canvas of Raphael with his works in the loggia of the Vatican, the first sign of his preoccupation with the idea of the artist, and a curious one; Raphael's landscape of his *casa* looked like a Claude, while Bernini's colonnade appeared in the background. The stony material of the Roman scene was the subject of a great and original picture, the *Forum Romanum*. The sunlit masonry is scattered, with the sense of natural litter that Ruskin remarked in Turner's foregrounds, under wide arches, which the reflected radiance makes lighter than the sky. One can see the effect any day in the South, yet it had hardly been noticed in painting since the primitives; Turner embraced it with evident delight. Colour and reflection were indeed precisely the properties of the world which were most to his purpose. They were the very essence of practicability, and he now turned to the systematic study of them. He rewrote his Academy lectures to emphasize them and illustrated their principles in drawings like the three included here.

Reflections occupied him far beyond the purposes of representation. The 'more minute investigation' of them, 'which may in the end discover positive axioms', became an end in itself, and a noble ambition. 'He that attains it will merit not only the thanks of those who follow him but will for himself build up a name that must be honoured as long as the English School' ('or as long as reflexies', Turner added) 'exists.' The ambition was characteristic; no artist ever had the three traditional motives of painting, fame, money and the love of art, in better balance than Turner. 'Anyone must be sensible,' he went on, 'How much has been done by Reflexies in the British School and how much remains to be done,' so that 'it becomes the peculiar study of our lives. . .' A torrent of words followed. The vocabulary seems to have come from the second book of Newton's *Optics* but the argument is repetitive and obsessive. It is a reverie on the indefinite transmission and dispersal of light by an infinite series of reflections from an endless variety of surfaces and materials, each contributing its own colour that mingles with every other, penetrating ultimately to every recess, reflected everywhere, 'plane to plane, so that darkness or total shade cannot take place while any angle of light reflected or refracted can reach an opposite plane'. Turner's axiom, in fact, amounted to a whole view of the world. . . 'We must consider every part as receiving and emitting rays to every surrounding surface. . .' It was not only a view of nature. The idea of the infinite interpenetration of natural radiance was necessarily also an idea of painting. Reading the lecture, we are already in the world of later nineteenth-century art, in which (as Felix Fénéon wrote in 1886) 'Every surface sends out colourations of various strengths which diminish and interpenetrate like widening ripples. . .'

One kind of reflection had a special significance for Turner. He became occupied with reflections in various metals with different degrees of polish. He was evidently interested in the precise conditions in which reflected light

A Storm. c. 1826. Watercolour, 12½ × 19″.
The British Museum, London

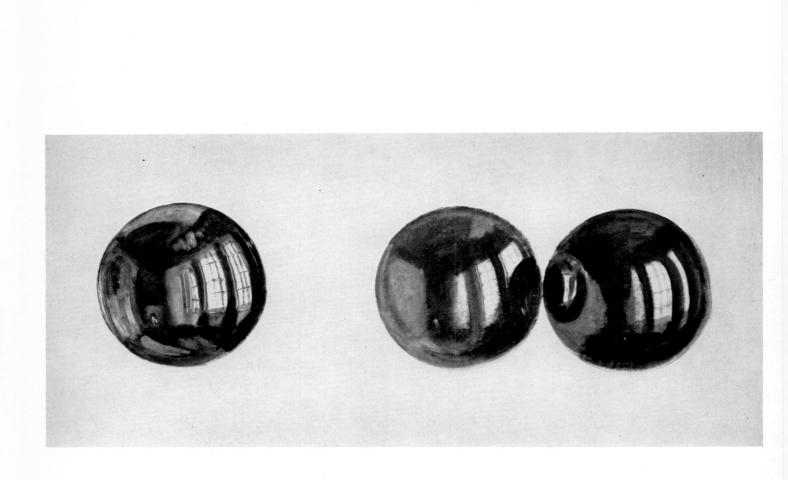

Reflecting Metallic Spheroids. c. 1820–8. Oil on paper, 25 × 38½″. The British Museum, London

became an image — in mirrors, in window panes and on the surfaces, exterior and interior, of spheres. Such images were demonstrably composed of light, and they were coloured by the medium in which they were seen. He observed them at length in nature and described their appearance in the old masters. One sheet of the illustrations that he made for the lecture showed light filtering through glass balls more or less filled with coloured liquids. Another showed his painting-room reflected on the convex surfaces of polished metallic spheres, which also reflect one another. The ostensible subject had evidently led him to another; he was preoccupied with circular images for their own sake. Turner was more at home than anyone with the rounded image of the topographical vignette. It was characteristic of him to become engrossed, almost incidentally, in the intrinsic visual nature of a convention and study it afresh. The idea that images could possess an inherent shape, and one that was not rectangular, reappeared many years later in some of his most original pictures.

Turner's view of colour was a similar combination of inherited knowledge with a highly personal attitude. His source was Moses Harris, the painter-entomologist, whose *Natural System of Colours*, commended by Reynolds, had been republished in 1811. Turner took Harris's colour circle and converted it to his own purpose in two diagrams. He had no use for the arrangement; he required yellow in the dominant position at the top, where Harris had red. The ring of 'primitive' and secondary colours round the circumference, with 'harmonizing' complementaries opposite one another, had evidently no significance in itself; he altered it by eliminating purple, a colour that he never cared for and moreover regarded as the enemy of yellow. In the centre of Harris's circle three triangles showed the mixture of the three primitive colours producing black. Turner supplemented his version of the diagram, which he marked No. 2, with quite a different one of his own, marked No. 1 and labelled in his notes Mixtures of Light. Yellow now occupied fully half of the circumference. The triangles were enlarged and arranged to show the mixtures of yellow with red and with blue, no darker than their constituents; the mixture of red and blue was naturally avoided. These were 'the pure combinations of the Aerial colours', as Turner called them; the second diagram showed the mixtures of 'dense material' colour.

They are the first diagrams of their kind by any artist of standing that we know. The distinction between mixtures of pigments and the constitution of light was well known but the directness of Turner's antithesis between the two types of mixture was original. The principle of additive and subtractive colour mixtures remained unknown until Helmholtz. Turner's eccentric anticipation of it was probably due to his own intuition. For him, the theory of colour held a profound imaginative richness:

White in prismatic order is the union or compound light, while the . . . mixture of our material colours

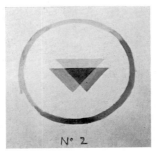

Colour Diagrams. After 1824. Watercolour, 21½ × 29½″. The British Museum, London

Death on a Pale Horse. c. 1830.
Oil, 23½ × 29¾″. The Tate Gallery, London

becomes the opposite; that is, the destruction of all, or in other words — darkness. Light is therefore colour and shadow the privation of it by the removal of those rays of colour, or subductions of power; and there are to be found throughout nature . . . the ruling principles of diurnal variations, the grey dawn, the yellow morning sun rise and red departing ray, in ever changing combination; these are the pure combinations of Aerial colours. . .

Turner knew the real character of the gulf between the colour of light and the colours of art, with a clarity which is rare among painters at any time. One can recognize in his pictures, particularly the pictures of yellow sunrise, not only purity of colour but a sense of tension, as if they recorded a continual aspiration towards an order of purity that is impossible in pigment. Moreover, the science of colour provided an explanation for the old precept which he had learnt from Fuseli, 'that one colour has a greater power than a combination of two' and 'a mixture of three impairs that power still more. . . ' Incorporating the words into his lecture, he added: '. . . and all beyond it monotony, discord, mud.' It was one of Turner's favourite remarks; many years later it was still in his mind and he noted it in the margin of Goethe's book on colour. Turner's approach was essentially empirical and practical; he was suspicious of systems. When Goethe, in Eastlake's translation, announced 'a development of all possible contrasts of the chromatic scale,' Turner's marginal comment was 'Off again, G.' For him, as he said at the end of his lecture, colour depended on

Nature and the perceptions of her effects; thro' all the mutability of time and seasons they are our materials and offered daily as our patterns of imitation, towards which we are assisted by each class of Theory a certain portion of our way. . .

Turner looked at the intrinsic visual character of painting with a directness that anticipated the studies of modern painters. But other events of the time were to contribute at least as much to the formation of the later style. One of the most significant developments was the most private; it is contained in three little sketchbooks, closed with metal clasps. One of the three already contained some pencil drawings of people fishing at a weir. His next use of the books was quite unconnected with them, or at first sight with anything else. Red and grey washes were swept across the pages, more and more broadly until leaf after leaf held torrents of sombre colour, tiny enigmatic cataracts. In two of the books naked figures begin to materialize out of the flux, and in one it becomes possible to construe the scenes. They are scenes of love in curtained beds, some passionate, others strangely desolate. The dark floods of tone were to become an essential element of Turner's later art, and they have an erotic meaning that was never displayed openly in pictures.

In one of the oil sketches that survive, the pressure of emotional experience is equally direct and urgent. The image that materializes out of drifting cloud and fire is

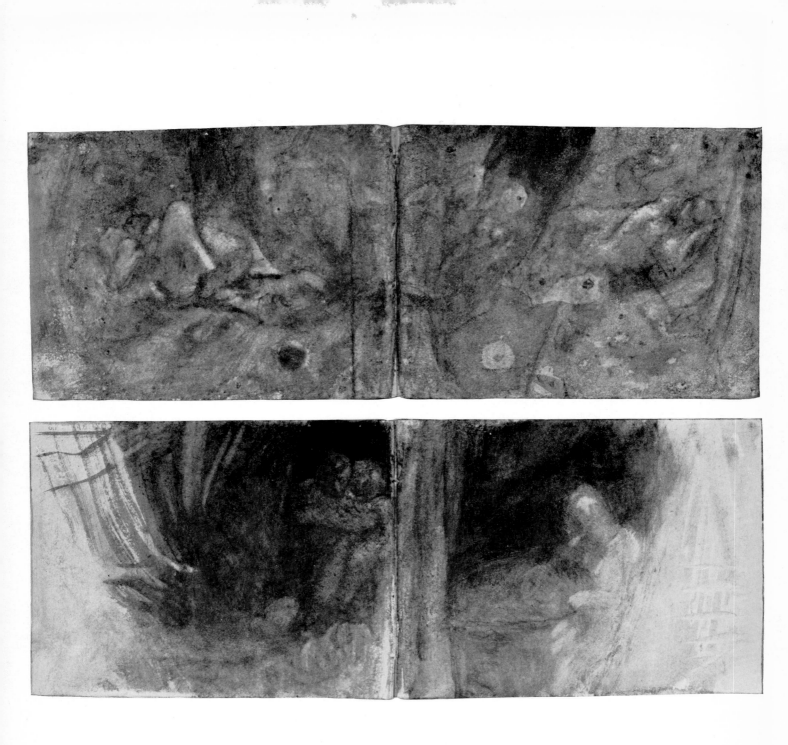

Sketchbook with Figures. c. 1830. Watercolour, 3 × 4″. The British Museum, London

Bedroom at Petworth. c. 1830.
Gouache on blue paper, 5½ × 7½″.
The British Museum, London

Petworth Park: Tillington Church in the Distance. c. 1830–1. Oil, 25½ × 58″. The Tate Gallery, London

apparently *Death on the Pale Horse*, from the Apocalypse. The rendering is unconventional and vivid; there is horror and tragedy in it. The sketch may possibly date from the time of the illness and the death in 1829 of Turner's father, who had been his companion and factotum all his working life. In the years after his father's death Turner stayed for long periods with his patron Lord Egremont at Petworth. The series of little gouaches in which he painted the life of the house — 'Everything solid, liberal, rich and English,' as Haydon described it — are his most purely delightful works. They flowed from his brush; he was at ease with the company, and the impromptu sketches, brushed directly in pale, liquid colour, had a lightness of tone and touch, and of mood as well. Turner's wit and his sociability in private hardly appeared in his art anywhere else, but the informality of his work at Petworth and the extempore freedom of his touch affected everything that he painted afterwards.

The grandeur of Turner's later painting is different in kind from the impressiveness of earlier years. In the finished sketch for one of the long pictures that he painted for the dining-room at Petworth, showing the park with Tillington church in the distance, there is only a vestige of the Claudian framework for evening landscape. The rays of the setting sun fan out across empty space. In place of artifice, there is the natural symmetry of light. It is the first sight both of the unhindered radiance of the later pictures and of a kind of structure which becomes particularly characteristic of his style ten years later. Light makes its own broadening path towards us; down across the meadow or lagoon or sea, dissolving the detail in its way, and upward '. . . measuring the wide concave of the circumambient air.' (Turner noted the words at the end of his lecture on colour). Many of his pictures after 1840 are similarly balanced on an incandescent central axis. It became one of his basic picture forms; indeed it is now so familiar that we can hardly see morning or evening light in any other shape. It was in fact a bold defiance of convention. The essence of the picturesque was asymmetry. *The Sketcher's Manual*, a guide to picturesque practice published in 1837, giving examples of compositions to be avoided, illustrated precisely the design of pictures like *A Yacht approaching the Coast*, as well as those of *Peace: Burial at Sea* and *Seascape*. The cone of sunlight in *Petworth Park* and its successors was designed to give radiance its natural symmetry. There is a Platonic geometry in it, which Turner no doubt recognised; in the course of his lectures he often quoted lines from Akenside describing how man guided by truth discerns

> In matter's mouldering structures, the pure forms
> Of Triangle, or Circle, Cube or Cone.

The grandeur of Turner's later pictures was sustained by a grand conception of the imaginative artist. He regarded painting as 'the most truly great and least appreciated' of the arts. Although he thought it his duty to teach, he had always in mind the uniqueness of creative genius as some-

Billiard Room at Petworth. c. 1830.
Gouache on blue paper, $5\frac{1}{2} \times 7\frac{1}{2}''$.
The British Museum, London

'The light . . . should never be so placed as to form a line,'
Compositions to be avoided, from *The Sketchers Manual*,
by Frank Howard. London, 1837*

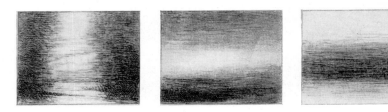

Monte Gennaro. 1819. Watercolour, 10 × 16″.
The British Museum, London

On the Coast. c. 1830.
Gouache on blue paper, 5½ × 7½″.
The British Museum, London

thing innate and unteachable, apart from skill. Towards the end of the eighteen-twenties the idea of the artist came to occupy him more and more. His public tribute to the great masters was characteristically eccentric. He painted pictures of them painting or incorporated their names in his titles. Watteau and Rembrandt provided the subject of costume-pieces; Canaletto was inserted in a magnificent view of Venice; Ruysdael was honoured by naming a non-existent Dutch port after him. They were not the painters who had been his original sources. They were chosen rather as examples of his own elevated conception of the artist's status, and his new ideal of painterly freedom and independence. Though his attitude to the masters always included an element of rivalry, he required from them real justification and support for all that seemed enigmatic and capricious in his own mastery. In lecture notes, which were surely never delivered, he described 'the utmost range of art . . . The imagination of the artist dwells enthroned in his own Recess, incomprehensible as from Darkness.'

His ideal of the artist was called on to justify his growing disdain for petty details, as well as for the customary descriptive conventions. They introduced arbitrary choices; painting for him was compulsive and absolute. All this is implied in his view of the artist's status. One account of it begins as disconnected jottings, then breaks into verse in the manner of Akenside:

High born soul — not to descend to any humble quarry — for amid the various forms which this fall would present
   Like rivals to his choice, what human breast
   E'er doubts, before the transient and Minute,
   To Prize the Vast, the Stable, the Sublime?

Turner's attitude to fame was always complex. As a young man he was already infinitely scornful of painters who did not aim high. A verse in one of his sketchbooks made fun of Wilkie for listening to flattery, and remaining content with Teniers. On the next page he copied out a flattering review of his own pictures. He had lately abandoned Wilkie's style, leaving unpainted a satire on a complacent artist using 'Stolen hints from celebrated pictures'. In 1828 it was Wilkie, over dinner in Rome, who impressed on Turner how regrettable it was 'that such a man as he could not feel the beauties of such an observer as Rubens'. Wilkie was at the time remodelling his style to imitate the 'black and powerful manner' of the later Italian and Spanish masters (anticipating the tonal historicism of French painting in the middle of the century). When the results were exhibited in the next year, Turner (as a critic said) was blazing and dazzling, and Wilkie's blackness was overshadowed; for a time there was a coolness between the two friends. The picture which Turner painted twelve years later in memory of Wilkie, *Peace: Burial at Sea*, has significant overtones of meaning (p. 30). It was not only a tribute to fame and friendship; it was also a sly demonstration of how to use black. It illustrated, no doubt deliberately, the distinction

The Pink Sky. After 1820. Watercolour 7¼ × 8⅞″. The British Museum, London

Peace — Burial at Sea. 1842. Oil, 24½ × 36½". The Tate Gallery, London

between natural effect and the imaginative reality of art. Stanfield, one of the generation that had learned aerial perspective from Turner's earlier style, remonstrated with him about the blackness of the sails and said that the colour and effect were untrue. Turner replied, 'I only wish I had any colour to make them blacker'.

There were countless stories of Turner's defiant response to criticism. His bluff and abrupt manner was defensive. To prize what was vast above what was minute ran against the whole trend of painting in the second quarter of the century. Yet his conception of the artist positively required it; he was compelled to appear defiant and perverse. After Mr. Lenox of New York had received a picture which heralded the later style, Turner met C. R. Leslie who had bought it for him:

> 'Well, and how does he like the picture?'
> 'He thinks it indistinct.'
> 'You should tell him that indistinctness is my forte.'

Turner rarely spoke of his works. Ruskin described him as 'generally, respecting all the movements of his own mind, as silent as a granite crest.' Almost the only thing he said about them was, 'Keep them together.' 'What is the use of them but together?' It was in the early eighteen-thirties that Turner made a will leaving the whole contents of his studio to the public, with a gallery to contain them. His consciousness of his role as an artist guided him in everything.

He found it confirmed above all by the example of Rembrandt. Twenty years earlier one of his comic genre pieces had been painted as a pendant to a Rembrandt, but when he turned to Rembrandt again, it was with a more serious sense of his significance. Turner expounded his view of Rembrandt in the lecture on landscape. 'Rembrandt', he said, 'depended upon his chiaroscuro, his bursts of light and darkness to be felt. He threw a mysterious doubt over the meanest piece of common —' (*Doubt* was one of Turner's favourite words; it was his own word for what Mr. Lenox called indistinctness.)

> —Nay more, his forms, if they can be called so, are the most objectionable that could be chosen . . . but over each he has thrown that veil of matchless colour, that lucid interval of morning dawn and dewy light on which the eye dwells so completely enthralled, and it seeks not for its liberty, but as it were thinks it a sacrilege to pierce the mystic shell of colour in search of form.

Whichever of the masters Turner wrote about, he was really writing about himself. He was using the past to reflect back his own view of the potentialities of painting. The pictorial counterpart of this passage was *Pilate washing his Hands*, which Turner exhibited in 1830. Ostensibly an imitation of Rembrandt, it was strangely original; it displayed for the first time the *veil of colour*, a glittering tissue of independent touches, out of which pictures like *Yacht Approaching the Coast* (p. 34) were to be created. Turner's words about

Shore and Sky. After 1820.
Watercolour, 8 × 10¾″. The British Museum, London

Rome Burning. c. 1834.
Gouache on brown paper, 8½ × 14½″.
The British Museum, London

The Slave Ship. 1840. Oil on canvas, 35¾ × 48″. The Museum of Fine Arts, Boston (Henry Lillie Pierce Fund)

Rembrandt are revealing; he imagined colour as a separate fabric, fragile and vulnerable, yet sacred and sufficient in itself to supply all the reality that is required from a picture.

The Petworth landscapes established the lasting character of the radiant, stable side of Turner's art. Then the other aspect reasserted itself, the tempestuous conflict of the elements. Mr. Lenox's picture was one of the first signs of it. But the forms which it took in Turner's ultimate achievement was largely due to one of the climactic experiences of his life. On an October night in his sixtieth year the Houses of Parliament were burnt to the ground. It is a sign of how much the fire at Westminster meant to Turner that he worked for once in colour direct from the subject (p. 14). He blotted the pages of his sketchbook one against another in his haste. A drama of flame and water on which he had brooded all his life was being acted out in reality in front of him.

His first uses of the subject in finished watercolours and the oil that is at Philadelphia were dramatic. They are like Romantic operas, with elaborate scenery and full chorus of horrified spectators. In the final painting at Cleveland, which is nearest to the sketchbook, the play of fire and its reflection in water were sufficient subject in themselves (frontispiece). He discovered a kind of equivalence between the experience and the picture for which his contemporaries were at a loss to account. It was far from descriptive; no one could forget that the picture looked like paint. It was not primarily even a record of light; critics pointed out that the night was more like day. The colour and the paint itself have an intrinsic reality of their own. We recognise in them an inherent meaning extending far beyond the actual scene.

A reviewer wrote in the next year of *Juliet and her Nurse* (p. 39): 'It is neither sunlight, moonlight, nor star-light, nor fire-light, though there is an attempt at a display of fireworks in one corner. . .' Turner was now concerned only with the inherent light that colour generates within a picture. To set it free he needed the homogeneous, diffuse consistency in which paint retains its own objective value. The reality of flame-like colour in *The Houses of Parliament* required complementary hues of almost equivalent tone. The effect of light which Turner noticed at sunset crossing the lagoon to Venice was similarly transposed into intervals of colour, the balanced, still fluorescence of orange-red against blue-green (p. 20). The classical sequence of tones was increasingly replaced by interactions of colour. The tonal order dissolved, and with it the classical pictorial structure. The diffuse consistency of colour evoked designs that spread outward from the centre. In Turner's sketchbooks and in his studio the expanding, interpenetrating colour was left with no graphic definition at all. When he died his studio was full of the images made by colour as if of its own accord.

In Turner's time they would hardly have been recognised as works of art. Fewer than half of the oils included here were exhibited during his life. Three years before his death Turner limited his bequest to finished pictures. Fortunately

Burning of the Houses of Parliament. 1834.
Watercolour, 17¾ × 11¾". The British Museum, London

The burning of the Houses of Parliament. 1835.
Oil, 36 × 48". The Philadelphia Museum of Art
(McFadden Collection).

Yacht approaching the Coast. c. 1840–5. Oil on canvas, 40½ × 56″. The Tate Gallery, London

Festive Lagoon Scene, Venice. c. 1840–5. Oil on canvas, 36 × 48½″. The Tate Gallery, London

Venice, the Piazzetta. c. 1835–7.
Oil, 36 × 48″. The Tate Gallery, London

Music at Petworth. c. 1835
Oil, 48 × 35½″. The Tate Gallery, London

the condition was set aside, for the evidence of what he regarded as finished is conflicting. He showed regularly in his last decade pictures that contemporaries thought unfinished and at least one of the early pictures that he reworked for exhibition was reduced to a state as amorphous as anything here. He probably knew a current saying that was ascribed to Rembrandt: 'A picture is finished when the artist has done with it.' Many painters of Turner's generation and the next were rebelling, as far as they could afford to, against the tyranny of finish. 'No room to get a thought in edgewise,' Giles said to Calvert, 'wretched work Sir!' Constable might not have thanked historians for attaching more significance to exhibition pictures, into which he put what he scornfully called eye-salve, than to those that he left without it. The note that Turner scribbled in the margin against Goethe's observation that the only completeness of painting lay in harmonious relations of tone and of colour was characteristically ironical: 'Yes — this is the true shot — but not winged the bird'. Goethe could not know how right he was.

The question of whether our interest in works that a painter kept unseen runs counter to his intentions can rarely be answered. Turner, who never lost an accident, was as aware of the enigma of artistic intention as we are; it lies near to the roots of art. Literature is defined as the activity of writers; it is perhaps only the institutional organisation of art that leads to any doubt that painting is simply what painters do. It is a kind of behaviour, with a pattern that can only be understood as a whole. Turner's concern that his work should be kept together betrays a realisation of precisely this, which was itself original. He was not the man to think that too much attention was paid to anything from his hand.

There is virtually no external evidence of when the pictures that he did not exhibit were painted. Nevertheless the outline of Turner's development in his last twenty years can be traced. The grand and formal drama of light and the elements which occupied Turner in the early eighteen-thirties appears in *A Rough Sea* (p. 20). In 1835, the year in which the versions of *The Burning of the Houses of Parliament* were exhibited, Turner visited Venice again. The patterns of positive colour in some of the drawings that he did there have a counterpart in the painting of *The Piazzetta*, in which the roof of the Doge's Palace was oddly embellished by one of the inspired accidents that Turner did not lose. The most richly patterned of the Petworth pictures, *The Music Party*, seems also to date from the middle years of the decade. In a painting of the same kind, *A Costume Piece*, what appears to be another party at Petworth takes on a strange solemnity as figures dressed like the models of Watteau and Van Dyck move in to dinner. *A Vaulted Hall* is more sombre; its massive design and handling has affinities with the *Val d'Aosta* (p. 52), exhibited in 1837, in which the alpine storm that had often been in Turner's thoughts broke with a darker savagery than ever. Sea-pieces with the natural delicacy of *Margate from the Sea* were perhaps painted in the eighteen-thirties.

Sunrise with a Boat between Headlands. c. 1835–40. Oil on canvas, 36 × 48¼″. The Tate Gallery, London

Sta. Maria della Salute and the Dogana, Venice. 1835?
Gouache on brown paper, 9½ × 12″.
The British Museum, London

Interior of a Wine Shop, Venice. 1835?
Gouache on brown paper, 9½ × 12″.
The British Museum, London

Towards the end of the decade light and colour became increasingly brilliant; the radiance of *A Boat between Headlands* (p. 37) almost submerges the relics of picturesque convention. The same cool light floods *Heidelberg* (p. 60), one of the pictures that embrace a scene as vast as the world-view landscapes of tradition. The visions of the world as an endless continuum are appropriately peopled with an almost indeterminate human clay, barely separated into individuals.

After 1840 the outward scene, which had been Turner's subject, was transformed; the essence of the drama was often inward and symbolic. The fantastic details of *The Slave Ship*, exhibited in 1840 (p. 32), were drowned in flooding colour. The interpenetration of light and the elements was embodied in forms that were boldly and freely invented, imaginary tongues of water and vapour like those in *Rockets and Blue lights*, (1840) which is at the Clark Institute at Williamstown. The corresponding picture here is *Yacht Approaching The Coast*, the loosest and most fragile of colour fabrics. *Snow Storm* (1842, p. 44) was a sweeping and original metamorphosis of form in movement; *Peace; Burial at Sea* (1842) represents the serene, elegiac aspect of the style. In the *Campo Santo: Venice* (1852, p. 55) from Toledo the transformation fuses reality with its reflections. The immensity of moving water forms the motive of the brooding *Seascape* (p. 57). In the two pictures suggested by Goethe, exhibited in 1843 (pp. 40 & 41), the same style is used for imaginative and symbolic purposes. The movement of weather and the train through space and light is the subject of *Rain, Steam and Speed* (1844, p. 48). The desolate, rocking movement of the emptiest and strangest of the seascapes, *Wreck with Fishing Boats* (p. 51), links it to the first half of the decade; drawings that are rather similar were dated in 1845. The watercolours that Turner brought back from his last continental tours, like *Buildings by a Lake* (p. 15), showed his view of the world in all its final gravity and richness, as a unity made out of correspondences of colour.

In the years that followed the restless tension relaxed. Reality and fantasy alike were gradually absorbed into light. The last scenes of Venice, in which barely perceptible gatherings of colour render the place and its floating life, may be near in date to *The Angel Standing in The Sun*, exhibited in 1846 (p. 54). The gentle ferocity of the *Sea Monster*, the fantastic embodiment of water, belongs to the same phase (p. 47). In two of the most evanescent canvases that remain an independent play of colour derives from storm and sunset at sea (p. 46). In 1850 Turner's last pictures, which remain underrated, included *Mercury sent to admonish Aeneas* (p. 49); it shows the serene resolution of his style.

Turner's pictures were always visibly and obviously made out of paint. In these last decades of his life the operation often took place in public. Nothing was more puzzling to his contemporaries than Turner's procedure with the pictures that he exhibited at the Academy. '. . . He used to send them in', the Redgraves wrote, 'in a most unfinished state, relying on what he could do for them during the

38

Juliet and her nurse. 1836. Oil, 35 × 47½″. Collection Mrs Flora Whitney Miller, New York

Shade and Darkness — the Evening of the Deluge. 1843. Oil on canvas, 30½ × 30½″. The Tate Gallery, London

Light and Colour (Goethe's Theory) — the Morning after the Deluge. 1843. Oil on canvas, 30½ × 30½″. The Tate Gallery, London

Thomas Fearnley: *Turner on Varnishing Day in 1837*
Oil on paper, 9⅛ × 9¼″. Collection N. Young Fearnley*

S. W. Parrott: *Turner on Varnishing Day in 1846*.
Oil on panel, 9⅞ × 9″. The Guild of St. George*

three days allowed to the members' for varnishing. '. . . He was generally one of the first to arrive, coming down to the Academy before breakfast and continuing his labour as long as daylight lasted; strange and wonderful was the transformation he at times affected in his works on the walls'. Robert Leslie, who was taken to the Academy as a boy by his father in the early eighteen-thirties, provided the most detailed description of Turner's technique that we have:

> There was no one, next to Stanfield and his boats, that I liked to get near so much as Turner, as he stood working upon those, to my eyes, nearly blank white canvasses in their old academy frames. There were always a number of mysterious little gallipots and cups of colour ranged upon drawing stools in front of his pictures; and, among other bright colours, I recollect one that must have been simple red-lead. He used short brushes, some of them like the writers used by house decorators, working with thin colour over the white ground, and using the brush end on, dappling and writing with it those wonderfully fretted cloud forms and the rippling and filmy surface curves upon his near water. I have seen Turner at work upon many varnishing days, but I never remember his using a maul-stick. He came, they said, with the carpenters at six in the morning, and worked standing all day. He always had on an old, tall beaver hat, worn rather off his forehead, which added much to his look of a North Sea Pilot. . . His colours were mostly in powder, and he mixed them with turpentine, sometimes with size, and water, and perhaps even stale beer, as the grainers do. . . Besides red-lead, he had a blue which looked very like ordinary smalt; this, I think, tempered with crimson or scarlet lake, he worked over his near waters in the darker lines.

In 1836 John Scarlett Davis wrote to a friend:

> . . . Turner has painted a large picture of 'The Burning of the Two Houses of Parliament', but I have heard it spoken of as a failure — a devil of a lot of chrome. He finished it on the walls the last two days before the Gallery opened to the public. I am told it was good fun to see the great man whacking away with about fifty stupid apes standing round him, and I understand he was cursedly annoyed — the fools kept peeping into his colour box, and examining all his brushes and colours.

E. V. Rippingille, who did not like Turner, gave a vivid description of the occassion:

> . . . Turner who, as he boasted, could outwork and kill any painter alive, was there, and at work at his picture, before I came, having set-to at the earliest hour allowed. Indeed it was quite necessary to make the best of his time, as the picture when sent in was a mere dab of several colours, and 'without form and void', like chaos before the creation. The managers knew that a

picture would be sent there, and would not have hesitated, knowing to whom it belonged, to have received and hung up a bare canvas, than which this was but little better. Such a magician, performing his incantations in public, was an object of interest and attraction. Etty was working by his side . . . and sometimes speaking to some one near him, after the approved manner of painters: but not so Turner; for the three hours I was there — and I understood it had been the same since he began in the morning — he never ceased to work, or even once looked or turned from the wall on which his picture hung. All lookers-on were amused by the figure Turner exhibited in himself, and the process he was pursuing with his picture. A small box of colours, a few very small brushes, and a vial or two, were at his feet, very inconveniently placed; but his short figure, stooping, enabled him to reach what he wanted very readily. Leaning forward and sideways over to the right, the left-hand metal button of his blue coat rose six inches higher than the right, and his head buried in his shoulders and held down, he presented an aspect curious to all beholders, who whispered their remarks to each other, and quietly laughed to themselves. In one part of the mysterious proceedings Turner, who worked almost entirely with his palette knife, was observed to be rolling and spreading a lump of half-transparent stuff over his picture, the size of a finger in length and thickness. As Callcott was looking on I ventured to say to him, 'What is that he is plastering his picture with?' to which inquiry it was replied, 'I should be sorry to be the man to ask him...' Presently the work was finished: Turner gathered his tools together, put them into and shut up the box, and then, with his face still turned to the wall, and at the same distance from it, went sidling off, without speaking a word to anybody, and when he came to the staircase, in the centre of the room, hurried down as fast as he could. All looked with a half-wondering smile, and Maclise, who stood near, remarked, 'There, that's masterly, he does not stop to look at his work; he *knows* it is done, and he is off.'

Turner was more secretive than anyone, but he had evidently an even stronger instinct for the nature of painting as a performance. His absorption in the intrinsic character of paint seems to have extended to the act of painting. It was as if he needed to exhibit an action as well as a picture. He gave a perennial demonstration of a quality in painting that he must have been determined should be recognised. It was like an anticipation of the recent controversy in New York about whether it is possible to hang an action on the wall, and a typically bluff and practical answer to it, which was none the less complete. The resulting pictures displayed a new kind of intrinsic, self-evident painting. They were visible demonstrations, which stand to this day, of 'the possibility of attaining what appears mysterious'.

Turner painting one of his pictures.
From *The Almanack of the Month*, June, 1846*

Snow Storm: Steamboat off a Harbour's Mouth. 1842. Oil on canvas, 36 × 48″. The National Gallery, London

There must have been other motives. No doubt Turner was half-reluctant to finish at all. The 'dab of several colours' was the equivalent in oil of the colour beginning in water-colour. Burnet described canvases prepared with patterns of blue and orange-yellow shading into brown. If they looked like *Landscape with Water* (p. 11), Turner's reluctance is comprehensible. Such canvases must have had the same kind of private value as the strips of watercolour in which he isolated the property of colour to constitute its own reality. His procedure at the exhibitions was a demonstration of the prior existence of the raw chromatic material, and of the ease with which form could be made out of it. One can imagine that the reality of colour was precious in itself, to be preserved until the last possible moment. In a canvas like *Sunrise: a Castle on a Bay* Turner seems to have taken one of his beginnings and given it, with the minimum of tenuous definition, its own kind of delicate, pearly substance. It seems to represent an intermediate stage between such pictures as *Sunrise with a Boat between Headlands*, in which the reality of colour with its own completeness was preserved intact, surely for his private purpose, and those which he exhibited.

The exhibition pictures were made of sterner stuff. One of the motives of the performances on the varnishing days was certainly to demonstrate the force that the intrinsic colour of painting possessed in his hands, overwhelming every other artist. They were the final manifestations of his power to outrival everyone, past and present. His contemporaries retaliated; soon the galleries were full of painters tuning up their pictures in competition and the rooms reverberated with colour. One of these encounters, recorded by C. R. Leslie, reveals the metaphoric force that colour possessed for English painters, and Turner's way of postponing to the last the translation of colour into form.

In 1832, when Constable exhibited his *Opening of Waterloo Bridge*, it was placed in the school of painting — one of the small rooms at Somerset House. A sea-piece, by Turner, was next to it — a grey picture, beautiful and true, but with no positive colour in any part of it. Constable's *Waterloo* seemed as if painted with liquid gold and silver, and Turner came several times into the room while he was heightening with vermilion and lake the decorations and flags of city barges. Turner stood behind him, looking from the *Waterloo* to his own picture, and at last brought his palette from the great room where he was touching another picture, and putting a round daub of red lead, somewhat bigger than a shilling, on his grey sea, went away without saying a word. The intensity of the red lead, made more vivid by the coolness of his picture, caused even the vermilion and lake of Constable to look weak. I came into the room just as Turner left it. 'He has been here,' said Constable, 'and fired a gun'. On the opposite wall was a picture, by Jones, of Shadrach, Meshach, and Abednego in the furnace. 'A coal,' said Cooper, 'has bounded across the room from Jones's picture, and set fire to Turner's sea.' The great man did not come again into the room for a day and a half; and then, in the last moments that were allowed for painting, he glazed the scarlet seal he had put on his picture, and shaped it into a buoy.

The Burning of the Houses of Parliament released a fantastic force in Turner's work. A barrier between reality and imagination had vanished; they were never distinct again. Fire became for a time a frequent subject and for the rest of Turner's life the incandescence of hot colour retained a fiery connotation. The fantasies were immense and pervasive. In later pictures the interaction of colour was often identified with flame and water. At other times the reference was simply to the colours of light and in canvases that remained in Turner's studio, like *Stormy Sea*, the play of colour and the elements leapt beyond the range or need of explanation. The distinction between hot and cold colour, traditional in studio teaching, occupied him continually. Drawing after drawing bears notes analysing it in every subject. Turner played the flute and there was perhaps a musical analogy; he thought of white as the top of the cold scale, yellow of the warm, and he made them both his special property. His infatuation with yellow became famous. There were endless jokes about it which he relished and added to. When he was thirty, he and his followers were already known as the White Painters; his touch was likened to a brush of snow. In his sketchbooks, white was a constant preoccupation. The fascination was connected with its well-known intractability to aerial perspective; Turner's notes were often reminiscent of the quotation from Du Fresnoy which he appended to his painting of Watteau:

> White, when it shines with unstained lustre clear,
> May bear an object back or bring it near.

It was also connected with Girtin, whose masterpiece, *The White House*, was a talisman to Turner. Over and over again he noted the title against a drawing, finally abbreviated to *W.H.*, as a reminder of the whiteness that transcended space.

Cold colour occupied Turner as long and as fiercely as hot. It held the terrors of sea and snow, and eventually the two were combined in a great picture. *Snow Storm* was the result of an event in Turner's life as crucial as the fire at Westminster. Again, a fantasy on which he had been brooding all his life became real. He recorded the fact in the catalogue: 'The author was in this storm on the night the Ariel left Harwich.' He treasured the experience like a private possession. When a friendly visitor to his gallery, the Rev. Kingsley, told Turner that his mother had liked the picture, Turner snubbed him, and gave us precious information:

> 'I did not paint it to be understood, but I wished to show what such a scene was like: I got the sailors to lash me to the mast to observe it; I was lashed for four

Sun Setting over the Sea. c. 1840–5. Oil on canvas, 36 × 48″. The Tate Gallery, London

Sunrise with a Sea Monster. c. 1840–5. Oil on canvas, 37½ × 47½″. The Tate Gallery, London

Rain, Steam and Speed. 1844
Oil, 35¾ × 48″. The National Gallery, London

Fort L'Ecluse from the Old Walls of Geneva. c. 1841
Watercolour and pencil, 9 × 11½″.
The British Museum, London

hours, and I did not expect to escape, but I felt bound to record it if I did. But no one had any business to like the picture.'

'But my mother once went through just such a scene, and it brought it all back to her.'

'Is your mother a painter?'

'No.'

'Then she ought to have been thinking of something else.'

There was a sense of compulsion, so intimate that he expected understanding to be confined to painters. Turner's very bearishness gives an impression of loyalty — to the experience, to the sea and the fear of it and also to his own vocation. Probably his story was precisely true; in any case the force of his reaction and his devotion were astonishing. He was sixty-six, but his imagination was again convulsed by the reality. The equation between fantasy and form was established afresh in a more dynamic shape than ever. The diffuse asymmetry of his image of peril was twisted again into the expanding spiral that was its most extreme and private form. He brooded on a critic's description of the paint as soap suds and whitewash: 'What would they have? I wonder what they think the sea's like? I wish they'd been in it.' *Snow Storm* is a picture of *being in it*. It had no reference to observation; Turner was in it, travelling in the ship he painted. He was in every sense the hero. It is a picture of his dream of endurance and defiance.

The movement of water, as Turner showed it, was also a movement of the eye and the image. Looking at *Snow Storm*, we lose our bearings with the ship. It is the beating of the paddle-wheel that churns the picture into its pitching, centrifugal shape. The momentum of *Snow Storm* is felt in the works of the years that followed. In the Goethe pictures the whole focus of the circular images is seen to be shifting and condensing. Turner himself was not sure if he had any business to like the intrinsic energy that was generated; these pictures were exhibited with the corners masked, hiding some of its most telling traces. Now that they are seen again entire as they appeared on his easel, they portray the movement of a pictorial process with extraordinary clarity.

Turner's art is full of images and traces of movement. He was alert to the kinetic force of painting; in his notes on pictures, 'a dark, dark sky' (in Poussin's *Pyramus*) or 'the knotted stems of trees' (in the *Peter Martyr*) were always *rushing*. The watercolours are often built out of parallel brush strokes with an inherent, energetic pattern. In the oils the parallel touches that render the light on a wave or a cloud, or on figures crossing the lagoon, portray the phases of a movement. Sometimes they are themselves created by the slipping, sticking motion of a palette knife. The vision of fantasy is in a continuous state of horizontal flux; the asymmetry of the *Sea Monster* is materializing and dissolving across the canvas as we look. In the eighteen-forties the linear movement of the style depended more and more on

Mercury Sent to Admonish Aeneas. 1850. Oil on canvas, 35 × 47″. The Tate Gallery, London

49

Margate from the Sea. c. 1835–40. Oil, 36 × 48″. The Tate Gallery, London

the lining brushes that Robert Leslie had noticed, which Turner had first used in the Petworth landscapes. The long transparent strokes portray connections that are more real than whatever was connected; they mark the directions of waves that have vanished or the gradations of light in the sky; they portray movements of the eye into distance.

Turner's engrossment in the heat and coldness of colours prepared him for the theories of Goethe, whose book was translated in 1840. Goethe divided his colour circle into two halves. Yellow, orange and red were called the 'plus' colours; 'the feelings they excite are quick, lively, aspiring'. On the other side were the 'minus' colours, blue-green, blue and purple, which produced 'a restless, susceptible, anxious impression.' Turner had always been sceptical about the emblematic connotations of colour, but the drama of Goethe's theory appealed to him. The minus colours were embodied in *The Evening of the Deluge* (p. 40) and the plus colours in the *Morning* (p. 41). He may not have forgotten his earlier source; the appearance of a beardless Moses at the Deluge is less surprising if Turner, an inveterate punster, had also in mind Moses Harris, to whom the genesis of colour studies in English art was due. The vortex into which Goethe's hues are whirling in the *Morning* is perhaps the 'pure combination of aerial colours'; in the *Evening* gross material colour makes darkness. There is annihilation of a kind in both the pictures. The equation that seems to have dictated the subject is significant. Colour and light were evidently identified with water and vapour.

Perhaps the whole essence of Turner's last works might be gathered from the compound, infinite meanings that he gave to water. It was not only, more often than not, his subject; it was in many senses his medium. Water typified the world as he imagined it, a world of rippling, echoing light. Long before, studying reflections, he had come to the reflecting and refracting medium which outshone everything; perhaps it had been the real object from the beginning. He turned in scorn on those who did not love water's 'liquid melting reflection', then, deserting optics, filled the margin with its beauties — colour; motion, clean or turbid, ever pleasing; the mountain stream struggling with impediments or spread in the unruffled lakes; the broad cerulean wave, calmly bright or lashed into foam and spray, overwhelming to the imagination; the power of the ocean — bursting out at last with the terrific apostrophe: 'Thou dreadful and tumultuous home of Death!'

If the Academy students ever heard these words, they must have been astonished. Perhaps Ruskin was right in thinking that Turner's deepest subject was death. Now that Turner's private achievement bulks so large, we are less concerned with the thread of Atropos, as Ruskin called it, than with the material richness that it entwined along the way. The pessimism was certainly present, but it possessed — not least in the extracts which Turner produced in the catalogues year by year from his fragmentary epic on the *Fallacies of Hope* — such ironic overtones that it may well be regarded as part of the sardonic protective front with which he

A Wreck with Fishing Boats. c. 1840–5.
Oil, 36 × 48″. The Tate Gallery, London

Storm Clouds: Looking out to Sea. 1845.
Watercolour and pencil, 9⅝ × 13¼″.
The British Museum, London

Snow Storm, Avalanche and Inundation in the Val d'Aosta. 1837. Oil, 36¼ × 48″. The Art Institute of Chicago (Frederick T. Haskell Collection)

guarded a private certainty of victory and fame. Robert Motherwell has spoken perceptively of the tragic quality in Turner's art, which painting seeks again now; in Turner the quality is perhaps as truly called heroic.

His audacity was a genuine courage. He was deeply aware of the terror of nature and mortality. He painted it, and the paint committed him. It was brave to make light and colour real. The tense purity of colour itself possessed a quality of the terrible. At the very beginning of his colour studies he made a note from Lomazzo, describing light as an emanation of the Deity. The threat of apocalyptic fury hung over all his work. Violence was an unflinching part of his palette. Recording the colour of clouds around the 'ensanguined sun,' he noted 'orpiment and blood', 'fire and blood,' as simple working information. In his twenties he had planned a subject from the Apocalypse, *The Water turn'd to Blood*. It could not be painted then; it was to be one of the basic themes of his life. The transmutation affected everything and it was achieved by colour and reflection. The subject from the Apocalypse in which it culminated, when Turner was seventy-one, was the most terrible of all. If we doubt the theme of *The Angel Standing in the Sun*, the words that Turner attached to the picture in the catalogue enforce it. Light is not only glorious and sacred, it is voracious, carnivorous, unsparing. It devours impartially, without distinction, the whole living world.

Water gave some of its meaning to watercolour. The wetness of the medium had fateful connotations. The colour of clouds, and eventually all colour, soaked out into it, bleeding and drowning. The wonder and terror of the moment are arrested and preserved in hundreds of drawings. The uncontrollable hazards of watercolour were the medium of Turner's private imaginative life. He was at home with them and trusted them, just as he trusted the rich, capricious deposit of oil paint. He made the chance and fate of painting his fate; he was content to abide by it. The diaphanous, yet strangely violent tissue of the last paintings holds a profound confidence and courage, a faithful agreement to conditions that are inherent not only in painting but in the whole irrevocable order of the material world.

Mercury Sent to Admonish Aeneas (p. 49) was one of Turner's last four pictures, all of Carthaginian subjects, exhibited in the year before his death. As colour becomes visible, it dilates on the canvas. The halation diffuses, tingeing the next, until every hue is present in every other, enriching yet also destroying. There is an illusion that colour is gathering in awesome caverns, places of simultaneous reconciliation and annihilation. This is Turner's conclusion, and it justifies Ruskin's insight: '. . . . Here and there, once in a couple of centuries, one man will rise past clearness and become dark with excess of light.'

After Turner's death the son of his old friend, the Rev. Trimmer, gained admittance to his studio:

This, during his lifetime, had been enshrined in mystery, and the object of profound speculation. What

A Lurid Sunset. c. 1840–5
Watercolour, 9¾ × 12″. The British Museum, London

Val d'Aosta. c. 1836.
Watercolour and pen, 9½ × 13½″.
The Art Institute of Chicago (Olivia Shaler Swan Fund)

The Angel standing in the Sun. 1846. Oil, 30½ × 30½″. The Tate Gallery, London

would his brother-artists have given some thirty years before to have forced an entrance when Turner was at the height of his fame! Often when shown into his gallery had I seen him emerge from that hidden recess. The august retreat was now thrown open; I entered. His gloves and neckhandkerchief lay on a circular table, which had in the middle a raised box (with a circle in the centre) with side compartments; a good contrivance for an artist, though I had never seen one of the kind before. In the centre were his colours, the great object of my attraction. I remember, on my father's observing to Turner that nothing was to be done without ultramarine, his saying that cobalt was good enough for him; and cobalt to be sure there was, but also several bottles of ultramarine of various depths; and smalts of various intensities, of which I think he made great use. There was also some verditer. The next object of interest was the white; there was a large bottle of blanc d'argent, and another of flake white. Before making this inspection I had observed that Turner used silver white. His yellow pigments consisted of a large bottle of chrome. There was also a bottle of tincture of rhubarb and some iodine, but whether for artistical or medicinal use I cannot say. Subsequently I was told by his housekeeper that ultramarine was employed by him very sparingly, and that smalt and cobalt were his usual blues. She was in the habit of setting Turner's palette. The palette — at least that in use, for he possessed two large splendid ones — was a homely piece of square wood, with a hole for the thumb. Grinding colours on a slab was not his practice, and his dry colours were rubbed on the palette with cold-drawn oil. The colours were mixed daily, and he was very particular as to the operation. If they were not to his mind, he would say to Mrs. Danby, 'Can't you set a palette better than this?' Like Wilson, Turner used gamboge; simply pounded and mixed with linseed cold-drawn oil.

His brushes were of the humblest description, mostly round hog's tools, and some flat. He was said to use very short handles, which might have been the case with his water colours; but I observed one very long-handled brush, with which I have no doubt he put in the effective touches in his late pictures. According to his housekeeper, he used the long brush exclusively for the rigging of ships, &c. However, there were a great many long-haired sables, which could not have been all employed for rigging. She also said that he used camel's hair for his oil pictures; and formerly he showed my father some Chinese brushes he was in the habit of using. When he had nearly finished a picture, she said, he took it to the end of his long gallery, and there put in the last touches.

I next inspected his travelling-box. Had I been asked to guess his travelling library, I should have said Young's *Night Thoughts* and Isaak Walton; and there they were, together with some inferior translation of

Campo Santo, Venice. 1842. Oil, 24½ × 36½″. The Toledo Museum of Art, Ohio (Gift of Edward Drummond Libbey).

Alpine Pass with Cascade and Rainbow. c. 1844.
Watercolour, pencil and pen, 8⅝ × 11¼".
The British Museum, London

Horace. His library was select, but it showed the man. A red morocco pocket-book, from the wear and tear it exhibited, one might have imagined to have been his companion through life. There were cakes of water-colour fastened on a leaf, the centres of which were worn away; the commonest colours, and one being a cake of verditer; one or two sable brushes and lead pencils, not in wood, with which he seemed to have drawn outlines in his sketch-book. These consisted of a few lines which he used to say no one could make out but himself. I have some doubts if he could have made them out himself without the assistance of other draw-ings; and he seems to have purchased detail views of foreign scenery, of which there was a large assortment well thumbed; the drudgery of the art, of which master minds avail themselves.

There is no doubt that in his early pictures he used wax, from their having turned yellow; there was a jar of wax melted with rose madder and also with blue, which must have been used very recently, though it might have been for water colours. There was also a bureau of old colours and oils, which I looked over very carefully; a bottle of spirit varnish and a prepara-tion of tar, tubes of magilp, old bladders of raw umber and other dark earths.

The above, with numerous unframed pictures around the apartment, were the contents of his paint-ing-room, which had no skylight. It had been origin-ally the drawing-room, and had a good north light, with two windows.

I must confess that a deep melancholy pervaded me as I made this inspection. Till of late years I had been in the habit of entering the house from my childhood; the owner was no more: he stood alone in the world, and his race was extinct.

Even twenty years ago it would not have been easy to disagree with Mr. Trimmer's conclusion. Now we find that a kind of painting, which is of vital concern to us, was anticipated by Turner. And by Turner alone; no one else before developed so far and with such devotion this special order of painting, which is so hard to define and yet so recognisable. It is hard to define because the fantasy and the image are implicit in the material it is made of, inseparable from the actual behaviour of paint in the painters hands. Turner showed that a certain potentiality was inherent in the nature of painting. The latent possibility has emerged again. Turner's vision and his towering fantasy remain his own, beyond compare. Nevertheless we meet him with a sense of recognition.

Seascape. c. 1840–5. Oil, 35¾ × 48″. The Tate Gallery, London

BIOGRAPHICAL NOTE

April 23rd, 1775 Joseph Mallord William Turner born in Covent Garden, London, son of a barber.
1789 Student at the Royal Academy Schools.
1790 First watercolours exhibited at the Royal Academy.
1796 First oil painting exhibited at the Royal Academy.
1799 Moved to lodgings in Harley Street. Elected an Associate of the Royal Academy.
1802 Elected a full Academician. Visited France and Switzerland, studying old masters in the Louvre.
1804 Opened a gallery at Harley Street to show his own pictures. Turner's mother died insane.
1806 Took a house by the river at Hammersmith.
1807 Elected Professor of Perspective at the Royal Academy. 'A Mrs Danby, widow of a musician, now lives with him.'
1810 Moved to Queen Anne Street, adjoining Harley Street.
1811 First series of lectures. Left Hammersmith, building a house at Twickenham.
1819 Rebuilt his house in Queen Anne Street, adding a new gallery.
August 1819–January 1820 First visit to Italy.
1828 Last series of lectures as Professor of Perspective.
1829 Death of Turner's father.
1830 A regular visitor to Petworth until Lord Egremont's death in 1837.
1837 Resigned the appointment as Professor of Perspective.
1840 Met Ruskin. Last visit to Venice.
1845 Last sketching tour abroad.
1846 Mrs Booth, housekeeper of a cottage in Cheyne Walk, Chelsea, which Turner had occupied for some years, mentioned in his Will.
1850 Exhibited for the last time at the Royal Academy.
December 19th, 1851 Died at Chelsea.

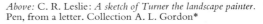

Above: C. R. Leslie: *A sketch of Turner the landscape painter.* Pen, from a letter. Collection A. L. Gordon*

Left: John Ruskin: *J. W. M. Turner R.A., as he was dressed for his visit to the opening of the Royal Academy.* Silhouette. Collection Richard Eurich*

CATALOGUE OF THE EXHIBITION

Turner's original titles for the pictures exhibited in his lifetime, together with the quotations that he attached to some of them, are quoted in full in this catalogue. These pictures were exhibited at the Royal Academy, unless otherwise indicated. Many of them are now generally known by the shorter titles used in the captions to illustrations in this book. The British national collections, which house the Turner bequest, are indicated, with catalogue numbers, as follows — N.G.: National Gallery. T.G.: Tate Gallery. B.M.: British Museum. T.B.: Inventory of the Drawings of the Turner Bequest, by A. J. Finberg, 2 vols, London, 1909.

Asterisk indicates illustrations of works not included in the exhibition.

In dimensions height precedes width.

Hill Town on the Edge of a Plain. 1828?
Oil, 16¼ × 23½″. The Tate Gallery, London

1 *Buttermere Lake, with part of Cromackwater, Cumberland, a shower.* Exh. 1798
'Till in the western sky the downward sun
Looks out effulgent — the rapid radiance instantaneous strikes
Th'illumin'd mountains — in a yellow mist
Bestriding earth — the grand ethereal bow
Shoots up immense, and every hue unfolds.'
Vide Thompson's Seasons.
Oil on canvas, 35 × 47″. T.G. 460. Ill. p. 6.

2 *The fifth plague of Egypt.* Exh. 1800
'And Moses stretched forth his hands towards heaven, and the Lord sent thunder and hail, and the fire ran along the ground.' — *Exodus, chap. ix. ver. 23.*
Oil on canvas, 49 × 72″. Art Association of Indianapolis, Herron Museum of Art. Ill. p. 8.

3 *Hill Town on Edge of Plain.* 1828?
Oil on linen on millboard, 16¼ × 23½″. T.G. 5526.

4 *Coast Scene near Naples.* 1828?
Oil on millboard, 16 × 23½″. T.G. 5527. Ill. p. 11.

5 *Death on a Pale Horse.* c. 1830
Oil on canvas, 23½ × 29¾″. T.G. 5504. Ill. p. 24.

6 *Petworth Park: Tillington Church in the Distance.* c. 1830–1
Oil on canvas, 25½ × 58″. T.G. 559. Ill. p. 26.

7 *Seashore with Two Horsemen.* c. 1830.
Oil on card, 8⅞ × 11¾″. B.M.

8 *A Rough Sea.* c. 1830
Oil on canvas, 36 × 48¼″. T.G. 1980. Ill. p. 20.

9 *The burning of the House of Lords and Commons, 16th of October, 1834.* Exh. British Institution 1835
Oil on canvas, 36 × 48″. Lent by the Commissioners of Fairmount Park, John H. McFadden Collection, Courtesy of the Philadelphia Museum of Art.

10 *The burning of the Houses of Lords and Commons, October 16, 1834.* Exh. 1835
Oil on canvas, 36½ × 48½″. The Cleveland Museum of Art, Ohio (John L. Severance Collection). Frontispiece.

11 *Music at Petworth.* c. 1835
Oil on canvas, 48 × 35½″. T.G. 3550. Ill. p. 36.

12 *Venice, the Piazzetta.* c. 1835–7
Oil on canvas, 36 × 48″. T.G. 4446. Ill. p. 36.

13 *A Costume Piece.* c. 1835–7
Oil on canvas, 35¾ × 48″. T.G. 5502.

14 *Juliet and her nurse.* Exh. 1836
Oil on canvas, 35 × 47½″. Mrs Flora Whitney Miller, New York. Ill. p. 39.

15 *Snow-storm, avalanche, and inundation — a scene in the upper part of Val d'Aout, Piedmont.* Exh. 1837
Oil on canvas, 36¼ × 48″. The Art Institute of Chicago (Frederick T. Haskell Collection). Ill. p. 52.

16 *A Vaulted Hall.* c. 1835–40
Oil on panel, 29½ × 36″. T.G. 5539.

17 *Margate from the Sea.* c. 1835–40
Oil on canvas, 36 × 48″. T.G. 1984. Ill. p. 50.

18 *Heidelberg.* c. 1835–40
Oil on canvas, 52 × 79¼″. T.G. 518. Ill. p. 60.

19 *Sunrise, with a Boat between Headlands.* c. 1835–40
Oil on canvas, 36 × 48¼″. T.G. 2002. Ill. p. 37.

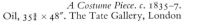

A Costume Piece. c. 1835–7.
Oil, 35¾ × 48″. The Tate Gallery, London

Heidelberg. c. 1835–40.
Oil, 52 × 79¼". The Tate Gallery, London

Whalers. 1846.
Oil, 36 × 48". The Tate Gallery, London

20 *Slavers throwing overboard the dead and dying — Typhon coming on.*
Exh. 1840
'Aloft all hands, strike the top-masts and belay;
Yon angry setting sun and fierce-edged clouds
Declare the Typhon's coming.
Before it sweep your decks, throw overboard
The dead and dying — ne'er heed their chains.
Hope, Hope, fallacious Hope!
Where is thy market now?' — *MS. Fallacies of Hope.*
Oil on canvas, 35¾ × 48". Museum of Fine Arts, Boston.
(Henry Lillie Pierce Fund). Ill. p. 32.

21 *Landscape with Water. c.* 1840–5
Oil on canvas, 48 × 71¾". T.G. 5513. Ill. p. 11.

22 *Yacht Approaching the Coast. c.* 1840–5
Oil on canvas, 40½ × 56". T.G. 4662. Ill. p. 34.

23 *Snow storm — steam-boat off a harbour's mouth making signals in
shallow water, and going by the lead. The author was in this storm on
the night the Ariel left Harwich.* Exh. 1842
Oil on canvas, 36 × 48". N.G. 530. Ill. p. 44.

24 *Peace — burial at sea.* Exh. 1842
'The midnight torch gleamed o'er the steamer's side,
And Merit's corse was yielded to the tide.' — *Fallacies of Hope.*
Oil on canvas, 32½ × 32½". T.G. 528. Ill. p. 30.

25 *Campo Santo, Venice.* Exh. 1842
Oil on canvas, 24½ × 36½". The Toledo Museum of Art, Ohio
(Gift of Edward Drummond Libbey). Ill. p. 55.

26 *Seascape. c.* 1840–5
Oil on canvas, 35¾ × 48". T.G. 4445. Ill. p. 57.

27 *Sunrise: A Castle on a Bay. c.* 1840–5
Oil on canvas, 36 × 48". T.G. 1985.

28 *Shade and darkness — the evening of the Deluge.* Exh. 1843
'The moon put forth her sign of woe unheeded;
But disobedience slept; the dark'ning Deluge closed around,
And the last token came: the giant framework floated,
The roused birds forsook their nightly shelters screaming,
And the beasts waded to the ark,' — *Fallacies of Hope, M.S.*
Oil on canvas, 30½ × 30½". T.G. 531. Ill. p. 40.

29 *Light and colour (Goethe's Theory) — the morning after the Deluge
— Moses writing the book of Genesis.* Exh. 1843
'The ark stood firm on Ararat; th' returning sun
Exhaled earth's humid bubbles, and emulsions of light,
Reflected her lost forms, each in prismatic guise
Hope's harbinger, ephemeral as the summer fly
Which rises, flits, expands, and dies.' — *Fallacies of Hope, M.S.*
Oil on canvas, 30½ × 30½". T.G. 532. Ill. p. 41.

30 *A Wreck with Fishing Boats. c.* 1840–5
Oil on canvas, 36 × 48". T.G. 2425. Ill. p. 51.

31 *Procession of Boats with Distant Smoke, Venice. c.* 1840–5
Oil on canvas, 35¼ × 47¼". T.G. 2068.

32 *Festive Lagoon Scene, Venice. c.* 1840–5
Oil on canvas, 36 × 48½". T.G. 4660. Ill. p. 35.

33 *Rain, Steam, and Speed — The Great Western Railway.* Exh. 1844
Oil on canvas, 35¾ × 48". N.G. 538. Ill. p. 48.

34 *Sun Setting over the Sea. c.* 1840–5
Oil on canvas, 36 × 48". T.G. 4665. Ill. p. 46.

35 *Stormy Sea. c.* 1840–5
Oil on canvas, 36 × 48". T.G. 4664.

36 *Sunrise, with a Sea Monster. c.* 1840–5
Oil on canvas, 35½ × 47½". T.G. 1990. Ill. p. 47.

37 *The Angel standing in the sun.* Exh. 1846
'And I saw an angel standing in the sun; and he cried with a loud
voice, saying to all the fowls that fly in the midst of heaven,
Come and gather yourselves together unto the supper of the
great God;
That ye may eat the flesh of kings, and the flesh of captains, and
the flesh of mighty men, and the flesh of horses, and of them
that sit on them, both free and bond, both small and great.' —
Revelation, xix., 17, 18.
'The morning march that flashes to the sun;
The feast of vultures when the day is done.' — *Rogers.*
Oil on canvas, 30½ × 30½". T.G. 550. Ill. p. 54.

38 *Whalers (boiling blubber) entangled in flaw ice, endeavouring to
extricate themselves.* Exh. 1846
Oil on canvas, 36 × 48". T.G. 547.

39 *Mercury sent to admonish Aeneas.* Exh. 1850.
'Beneath the morning mist,
Mercury waited to tell him of his neglected fleet.' — MS.
Fallacies of Hope.
Oil on canvas, 35 × 47". T.G. 553. Ill. p. 49.

Sunrise at Sea. After 1820.
Watercolour, 11½ × 15½".
The British Museum, London.

40 *San Giorgio from the Dogana, Venice: Sunrise.* 1819
Watercolour, 8 13⁄16 × 11 13⁄16". B.M. (T.B. CLXXXI–4). Ill. p. 12.

41 *Venice, Looking East from the Giudecca at Sunrise.* 1819
Watercolour, 8 13⁄16 × 11 13⁄16". B.M. (T.B. CLXXXI–5). Ill. p. 16.

42 *Como and Venice Sketchbook,* with colour beginnings. 1819
8⅞ × 11⅜". B.M. (T.B. CLXXXI).

43 *Monte Gennaro, near Rome.* 1819
Watercolour, 10 × 16". B.M. (T.B. CLXXXVII–41). Ill. p. 28.

44 *Storm Clouds: Sunset.* c. 1820
Watercolour, 9½ × 13¼". B.M. (T.B. CXCVII–F).

45 *A Storm.* c. 1826
Watercolour, 12½ × 19". B.M. (T.B. CCLXIII–41). Ill. p. 21.

46 *Sunrise at Sea.* After 1820
Watercolour, 11½ × 15½". B.M. (T.B. CCLXIII–68).

47 *Sunset on the Coast.* c. 1828
Watercolour, 12 × 19". B.M. (T.B. CCLXIII–87).

48 *A Rocky Coast.* After 1820
Watercolour, 11½ × 19". B.M. (T.B. CCLXIII–90).

49 *The Pink Sky.* After 1820
Watercolour, 7¼ × 8⅞". B.M. (T.B. CCLXIII–289). Ill. p. 29.

50 *Shore and Sky.* After 1820
Watercolour and pencil, 8 × 10¾". B.M. (T.B. CCLXIII–356).
Ill. p. 31.

51 *Reflecting Metallic Spheroids*
Oil on paper, 25 × 38½". B.M. (T.B. CXCV–176). Ill. p. 22.

52 *Colour Diagram No. 1.* After 1824
Watercolour, 21½ × 29½". B.M. (T.B. CXCV–178). Ill. p. 23.

53 *Colour Diagram No. 2.* After 1824
Watercolour, 21½ × 29½". B.M. (T.B. CXCV–179). Ill. p. 23.

54 *Sketchbook with Figures*. *c*. 1830
$3 \times 4''$. B.M. (T.B. CCXCI (b)). Ill. p. 25.

55 *Roadway at Petworth*. *c*. 1830
Gouache on blue paper, $5\frac{1}{2} \times 7\frac{1}{2}''$. B.M. (T.B. CCXLIV–53),

56 *Trees at Petworth*. *c*. 1830
Gouache on blue paper, $5\frac{1}{2} \times 7\frac{1}{2}''$. B.M. (T.B. CCXLIV–55).

57 *Trees at Petworth*. *c*. 1830
Gouache on blue paper, $5\frac{1}{2} \times 7\frac{1}{2}''$. B.M. (T.B. CCXLIV–56).

58 *Interior at Petworth with Two Seated Female Figures*. *c*. 1830
Gouache on blue paper, $5\frac{1}{2} \times 7\frac{1}{2}''$. B.M. (T.B. CCXLIV–78).

59 *Interior at Petworth with Figure in Yellow*. *c*. 1830.
Gouache on blue paper, $5\frac{1}{2} \times 7\frac{1}{2}''$. B.M. (T.B. CCXLIV–80).

60 *Interior at Petworth with Figures*. *c*. 1830
Gouache on blue paper, $5\frac{1}{2} \times 7\frac{1}{2}''$. B.M. (T.B. CCXLIV–81).

61 *Interior at Petworth*. *c*. 1830
Gouache on blue paper, $5\frac{1}{2} \times 7\frac{1}{2}''$. B.M. (T.B. CCXLIV–112).

62 *Bedroom at Petworth*. *c*. 1830
Gouache on blue paper, $5\frac{1}{2} \times 7\frac{1}{2}''$. B.M. (T.B. CCXLIV–115).
Ill. p. 26.

63 *Billiard Room at Petworth*. *c*. 1830
Gouache on blue paper, $5\frac{1}{2} \times 7\frac{1}{2}''$. B.M. (T.B. CCXLIV–116).
Ill. p. 27.

64 *Porte St. Denis*. *c*. 1830
Gouache on blue paper, $5\frac{1}{2} \times 7\frac{1}{2}''$. B.M. (T.B. CCLIX–6).

65 *Aux Invalides*. *c*. 1830
Gouache on blue paper, $5\frac{1}{2} \times 7\frac{1}{2}''$. B.M. (T.B. CCLIX–7).

66 *St. Laurent*. *c*. 1830
Gouache on blue paper, $5\frac{1}{2} \times 7\frac{1}{2}''$. B.M. (T.B. CCLIX–9).

67 *Group of Buildings*. *c*. 1830
Gouache on blue paper, $5\frac{1}{2} \times 7\frac{1}{2}''$. B.M. (T.B. CCLIX–38).

68 *An Open Place with Buildings*. *c*. 1830
Gouache on blue paper, $5\frac{1}{2} \times 7\frac{1}{2}''$. B.M. (T.B. CCLIX–39).

69 *On the Coast*. *c*. 1830
Gouache on blue paper, $5\frac{1}{2} \times 7\frac{1}{2}''$. B.M. (T.B. CCLIX–42). Ill. p. 28.

70 *Burning of the Houses of Parliament Sketchbook* (I). 1834
$9\frac{1}{4} \times 12\frac{3}{4}''$. B.M. (T.B. CCLXXXIII). Ill. p. 14.

71 *Burning of the Houses of Parliament*. 1834
Watercolour, $17\frac{3}{4} \times 11\frac{3}{4}''$. B.M. (T.B. CCCLXIV–373). Ill. p. 33.

72 *Rome Burning*. *c*. 1834
Gouache on brown paper, $8\frac{1}{2} \times 14\frac{1}{2}''$. B.M. (T.B. CCCLXIV–370).
Ill p. 31..

73 *Sunset, Returning from Torcello*. 1835?
Watercolour, $9\frac{1}{2} \times 11\frac{7}{8}''$. B.M. (T.B. CCCXVI–25). Ill. p. 17.

74 *Moonlight, Venice*. 1835?
Watercolour, $9\frac{11}{16} \times 12''$. B.M. (T.B. CCCXVI–39).

75 *A Procession, Venice*. 1835?
Gouache on brown paper, $9\frac{1}{2} \times 12''$. B.M. (T.B. CCCXVIII–14).

76 *Murder Scene, Venice*. 1835?
Gouache on brown paper, $9\frac{1}{2} \times 12''$. B.M. (T.B. CCCXVIII–17).

77 *Interior of a Wine Shop, Venice*. 1835?
Gouache on brown paper, $9\frac{1}{2} \times 12''$. B.M. (T.B. CCCXVIII–21).
Ill. p. 38.

78 *Interior with Figures, Venice*. 1835?
Gouache on brown paper, $9\frac{1}{2} \times 12''$. B.M. (T.B. CCCXVIII–25).

79 *Sta. Maria della Salute and the Dogana, Venice*. 1835?
Gouache on brown paper. $9\frac{1}{2} \times 12''$. B.M. (T.B. CCCXVIII–29).
Ill. p. 38.

80 *Lucerne*. *c*. 1835
Watercolour, $9\frac{3}{16} \times 11\frac{1}{2}''$. The Art Institute of Chicago (Gift of Margaret Mower in memory of her Mother, Elsa Durand Mower).

81 *Val d'Aosta*. *c*. 1836
Watercolour and pen, $9\frac{1}{2} \times 13\frac{1}{2}''$. The Art Institute of Chicago (Olivia Shaler Swan Fund). Ill. p. 53.

82 *Study of Fish*. *c*. 1839
Watercolour, $8\frac{3}{4} \times 13''$. B.M. (T.B. CCCLIII–22).

83 *The Arsenal, Rio di San Daniele, Venice*. 1840
Watercolour, $9\frac{5}{8} \times 12\frac{1}{8}''$. B.M. (T.B. CCCXVI–27).

84 *Lake with Distant Headland and Palaces*. *c*. 1840
Watercolour, $26\frac{1}{4} \times 39\frac{1}{4}''$. B.M. (T.B. CCCLXV–29).

85 *Boats at Sea*. *c*. 1840–5
Watercolour, $9\frac{3}{4} \times 12''$. B.M. (T.B. CCCLXIV–82).

86 *A Lurid Sunset*. *c*. 1840–5
Watercolour, $9\frac{3}{4} \times 12''$. B.M. (T.B. CCCLXIV–84). Ill. p. 53.

87 *Mount Pilatus*. *c*. 1840–5
Watercolour, $9\frac{3}{4} \times 14\frac{1}{2}''$. B.M. (T.B. CCCLXIV–198).

88 *A Beginning*. *c*. 1840–5.
Watercolour, $9\frac{3}{4} \times 14\frac{1}{2}$. B.M. (T.B. CCCLXIV–199).

89 *Fort L'Ecluse from the Old Walls of Geneva*. *c*. 1841
Watercolour and pencil, $9 \times 11\frac{1}{2}''$. B.M. (T.B. CCCXXXII–11).

90 *Ehrenbreitstein*. *c*. 1842–4.
Watercolour and pen, $9\frac{3}{4} \times 11\frac{15}{16}''$. B.M. (T.B. CCCLXIV–285).

91 *Alpine Pass with Cascade and Rainbow*. *c*. 1844.
Watercolour, pencil, and pen, $8\frac{5}{8} \times 11\frac{1}{4}''$. B.M.
(T.B. CCCLXIV–278). Ill. p. 56.

92 *Clearing Up*. 1845
Inscribed '12 May 45'.
Watercolour and pencil, $9\frac{3}{8} \times 13\frac{1}{4}''$. B.M. (T.B. CCCLVII–3).

93 *Looking out to Sea: a Whale Aground*. 1845
Inscribed 'I shall use this.'
Watercolour and pencil, $9\frac{3}{8} \times 13\frac{1}{4}''$. B.M. (T.B. CCCLVII–6).

94 *Sunset, Ambleteuse*. 1845
Watercolour and pencil, $9\frac{3}{8} \times 13\frac{1}{4}''$. B.M. (T.B. CCCLVII–9).

95 *Storm Clouds: Looking out to Sea*. 1845
Watercolour and pencil, $9\frac{3}{8} \times 13\frac{1}{4}''$. B.M. (T.B. CCCLVII–11).

96 *Storm Clouds: Looking out to Sea*. 1845
Watercolour and pencil, $9\frac{3}{8} \times 13\frac{1}{4}''$. B.M. (T.B. CCCLVII–12).
Ill. p. 51.

97 *Eu, with Louis Philippe's Chateau*. 1845
Watercolour, pen and pencil, $9\frac{1}{16} \times 12\frac{3}{4}''$. B.M. (T.B. CCCLIX–12).

98 *White Cliffs, Eu*. 1845
Watercolour and pencil, $9\frac{1}{16} \times 12\frac{3}{4}''$. B.M. (T.B. CCCLIX–14).

99 *Buildings by a Lake*. 1845
Watercolour and pencil, $9\frac{1}{16} \times 12\frac{3}{4}''$. B.M. (T.B. CCCLIX–18).
Ill. p. 15.

Lucerne. *c*. 1835. Watercolour, $9\frac{3}{16} \times 11\frac{1}{2}''$.
The Art Institute of Chicago
(Gift of Margaret Mower in memory of her mother
Elsa Durand Mower)

SELECTED BIBLIOGRAPHY

A selection of the most useful books on Turner is listed in order of date of publication. Fuller bibliographies are given by Finberg (bibl. 7), Butlin (bibl. 8), and Rothenstein and Butlin (bibl. 11). The manuscripts of Turner's lectures are preserved in the British Museum, Add MS. 46151. The lecture on Reflection and Colour is quoted from Box 1, MS. VIII and that on Landscape from Ziff (bibl. 41). Turner's annotated copies of Opie's *Lectures in Painting* (1810) and Goethe's *Theory of Colour*, translated by Eastlake, (1840) are in the collection of Mr C. W. Mallord Turner.

Murder Scene, Venice. 1835?
Gouache on brown paper, 9½ × 12″.
The British Museum, London

Study of Fish. c. 1839.
Watercolour, 8¾ × 13″. The British Museum, London

BOOKS

1 RUSKIN, JOHN. Modern Painters. 5 vols. London, Smith, Elder & Co., 1843–60.
2 BURNET, JOHN. Turner and His Works. London, David Bogue, 1852. 2nd. ed., London, James S. Virtue, 1859. With a 'Memoir' by Peter Cunningham.
3 THORNBURY, WALTER. Life of J. M. W. Turner, R.A. 2 vols., London, Hurst & Blackett, 1862. 2nd. ed., 1 vol., London, Chatto & Windus, 1877.
4 FINBERG, A. J. Turner's Sketches and Drawings. London, Methuen & Co., 1910.
5 ASHBY, THOMAS. Turner's Visions of Rome. London, Halton & Truscott Smith; New York, Minton, Balch & Co., 1925.
6 FINBERG, A. J. In Venice with Turner. London, The Cotswold Gallery, 1930.
7 FINBERG, A. J. The Life of J. M. W. Turner, R.A. Oxford, Clarendon Press, 1939, 2nd. ed., revised by Hilda F. Finberg, 1961.
8 BUTLIN, MARTIN. Turner Watercolours. London, Barrie and Rockliff, 1962; New York, Watson-Guptill Publications, 1965.
9 STOKES, ADRIAN. 'The Art of Turner (1775–1851)' in Painting and the Inner World. London, Tavistock Publications, 1963.
10 KITSON, MICHAEL. Turner. London, Blandford Press, 1964.
11 ROTHENSTEIN, JOHN and MARTIN BUTLIN. Turner. London, Heinemann, 1964, The Reprint Society, 1965.

ARTICLES SINCE 1946

12 BECKETT, R. B. 'Kilgarren Castle': a link between Turner and Wilson. *The Connoisseur* CXX no. 505: 10–15 ill. Sept. 1947.
13 BOASE, T. S. R. English Artists and the Val d'Aosta. *Journal of the Warburg and Courtauld Institutes* XIX: 283–93 ill. July 1956.
14 BOASE, T. S. R. Shipwrecks in English Romantic Painting. *Journal of the Warburg and Courtauld Institutes* XXII nos. 3–4: 332–46 ill. July–Dec. 1959.
15 CLARK, SIR KENNETH. Turner at Petworth. *The Ambassador* 8: 75–90 ill. 1949.
16 CUNNINGHAM, C. C. 'Van Tromp's shallop, at the entrance of the Scheldt'. *Wadsworth Atheneum Bulletin* 2nd. s. no. 30: 1 ill. Feb. 1952.
17 CUNNINGHAM, C. C. Turner's Van Tromp Paintings. *The Art Quarterly* XV: 322–30 ill. Winter 1952.
18 FINBERG, HILDA F. Turner's Gallery in 1810. *The Burlington Magazine* XCIII no. 585: 383–6 ill. Dec. 1951.
19 FINBERG, HILDA F. Turner's Views of Caernarvon Castle. *The Connoisseur* CXXIX no. 525: 32, 58 ill. March 1952.
20 FINBERG, HILDA F. 'Turner to Mr. Dobree'. Two Unrecorded Letters. *The Burlington Magazine*. XCV no. 600: 98–9. March 1953.
21 FINBERG, HILDA F. 'With Mr. Turner in 1797'. *The Burlington Magazine* XCIX no. 647: 48–51 ill. Feb. 1957.
22 FRANCIS, H. S. A Water Color by J. M. W. Turner ('Flüelen, Lake of Lucerne'). *The Bulletin of the Cleveland Museum of Art* 41 no. 9: 201–3 ill. Nov. 1954.
23 GAGE, JOHN. Turner and the Society of Arts. *The Journal of the Royal Society of Arts* CXI: 842–6 ill. Sept. 1963.
24 GAGE, JOHN. Magilphs and Mysteries. *Apollo* LXXX n. s. no. 29: 38–41 ill. July 1964.
25 GAGE, JOHN. Turner and the Picturesque. *The Burlington Magazine* CVII no. 742: 16–25 ill. Jan. 1965, no. 743: 75–81 ill. Feb. 1965.

26 GAUNT, WILLIAM. George Dance's Royal Academy. *The Connoisseur* 153: 182–6 ill. July 1963.

27 GOWING, LAWRENCE. Turner's 'pictures of nothing'. *Art News* 62: 30–3 ill. Oct. 1963.

28 GRAHAM, ANDREW. A National Gallery controversy of a century ago and its disastrous consequences for the Turner Bequest. *The Connoisseur* special no.: 14–17 ill. June 1959.

29 GUNTHER, CHARLES F. Landscapes of Fancy and Freedom. *The Toledo Museum of Art: Museum News* n. s. 3 no. 2: 37–40 ill. Spring 1960.

30 HANSON, N. W. Some Painting Materials of J. M. W. Turner. *Studies in Conservation* I: 162–73 ill. Oct. 1954.

31 KITSON, MICHAEL. Snowstorm: Hannibal Crossing the Alps. *Painting of the Month*: 73–6 ill. Aug. 1965, and *The Listener* LXXIV no. 1898: 240–1 ill. Aug. 12, 1965.

32 LIVERMORE, ANN. Turner and Music. *Music and Letters* 38 no. 2: 170–9 ill. April 2, 1957.

33 LIVERMORE, ANN. J. M. W. Turner's unknown verse-book. *The Connoisseur Year Book*: 78–86 ill. 1957.

34 PIPER, JOHN. English Painting at the Tate. *The Burlington Magazine* LXXXIX no. 535: 285. Oct. 1947.

35 QUENNELL, PETER. Petworth. *L'Oeil* 83: 38–45 ill. Nov. 1961.

36 VIRCH, CLAUS. 'Ye Mists and Exhalations That Now Rise'. *The Metropolitan Museum of Art Bulletin* n. s. XX no. 8: 248–56 ill. April 1962.

37 WALKER, RICHARD. The Third Earl of Egremont, Patron of the Arts. *Apollo* LVII no. 335; 11–13 ill. Jan. 1953.

38 WARNER, OLIVER. Turner and Trafalgar. *Apollo* LXII no 3682; 104 ill. Oct. 1955.

39 WILLETTS, PAMELA. Letters of J. M. W. Turner. *British Museum Quarterly* XXII nos. 3–4: 59–62 ill. April 1960.

40 ZIFF, JERROLD. Turner and Poussin. *The Burlington Magazine* CV no. 724: 315–21 ill. July 1963.

41 ZIFF, JERROLD. 'Backgrounds, Introduction of Architecture and Landscape': a Lecture by J. M. W. Turner. *Journal of the Warburg and Courtauld Institutes* XXVI: 124–47. 1963.

42 ZIFF, JERROLD. Proposed Studies for a Lost Turner Painting. *The Burlington Magazine* CVI no. 736: 328–33 ill. July 1964.

43 ZIFF, JERROLD. J. M. W. Turner on Poetry and Painting. *Studies in Romanticism* III no. 4: 193–215 ill. Summer 1964.

44 ZIFF, JERROLD. John Langhorne and Turner's 'Fallacies of Hope'. *Journal of the Warburg and Courtauld Institutes* XXVIII: 340–2. 1964.

45 ZIFF, JERROLD. Copies of Claude's Paintings in the Sketch Books of J. M. W. Turner. *Gazette des Beaux Arts* LXV no. 1: 51–64 ill. Jan. 1965.

EXHIBITIONS SINCE 1946

46 ADELAIDE, SYDNEY, MELBOURNE, BRISBANE and PERTH. An Exhibition of Paintings by J. M. W. Turner, R.A. Lent by the Tate Gallery. March–Sept. 1960. 16 exhibits.

47 AMSTERDAM, STEDELIJK MUSEUM. Turner. 1947. Organized by the Tate Gallery and the British Council. 68 exhibits.

48 BERNE, KUNSTMUSEUM. William Turner. Dec. 29, 1947–Feb. 1, 1948. Organized by the Tate Gallery and the British Council. 102 exhibits.

49 BRUSSELS, PALAIS DES BEAUX ARTS and LUIK, MUSEUM VOOR SCHONE KUNSTEN. Turner. March–April 1948. Organized by the Tate Gallery and the British Council. 67 exhibits.

50 DÜSSELDORF, WIESBADEN, MANNHEIM, MUNICH and NUREMBERG. Aquarelle aus dem Turner — Nachlass im Britischen Museum. Oct. 1950–March 1951. Organized by the British Council. 37 exhibits.

51 HONG KONG. THE CITY HALL ART GALLERY. Turner. An Exhibition of Watercolours from the British Museum. Jan. 3–29, 1964. Organized by the British Council. 50 exhibits.

52 INDIANAPOLIS, JOHN HERRON ART MUSEUM. Turner in America. Nov. 12–Dec. 25, 1955. 61 exhibits.

53 KING'S LYNN. Exhibition of Water Colours by J. M. W. Turner, R.A. July 27–Aug. 10, 1957. 28 exhibits.

54 LEEDS, CITY ART GALLERY. Turner Watercolours from Farnley Hall. Jan. 31–Feb. 28, 1948. 43 exhibits.

55 LONDON, THOS. AGNEW & SONS LTD. Centenary Loan Exhibition of Water-Colour Drawings by J. M. W. Turner, R.A. Feb.–March, 1951. 125 exhibits.

56 LONDON, THE ARTS COUNCIL OF GREAT BRITAIN. J. M. W. Turner, R.A. A selection of twenty-four oil paintings from the Tate Gallery. 1952. Travelling exhibition. 24 exhibits.

57 LONDON, LEGGATT BROTHERS LTD. J. M. W. Turner, R.A. Oct. 14–Nov. 4, 1960. 36 exhibits.

58 LONDON, THE TATE GALLERY. The Turner Collection from Petworth. May–July 1951. 18 exhibits.

59 LONDON, WHITECHAPEL ART GALLERY. J. M. W. Turner, R.A. Feb. 5–March 15, 1953. 224 exhibits.

61 MANCHESTER, CITY ART GALLERY. Water Colours by J. M. W. Turner, R.A. Dec. 10, 1952–Jan. 28, 1953. 77 exhibits.

62 MELBOURNE, NATIONAL GALLERY OF VICTORIA and SYDNEY, ART GALLERY OF NEW SOUTH WALES. J. M. W. Turner. Watercolours. Sept. 21–Oct. 1, and Oct.–Nov. 1961. 40 exhibits.

63 NEW YORK, OTTO GERSON GALLERY. Joseph Mallord William Turner. Watercolors and Drawings. Nov. 9–Dec. 10, 1960. 44 exhibits.

64 NOTRE DAME, INDIANA, THE ART GALLERY, UNIVERSITY OF NOTRE DAME. Turner in Indiana. Feb. 3–24, 1963. 53 exhibits.

65 PARIS, MUSÉE DE L'ORANGERIE. Turner. 1948. Organized by The Tate Gallery and The British Council. 67 exhibits.

66 ROME, MUSEO DI PALAZZO VENEZIA. Turner. 1948. Organized by The Tate Gallery and The British Council. 50 exhibits.

67 SAN MARINO, CALIFORNIA, HENRY HUNTINGDON ART GALLERY. Exhibition of Turner Watercolours. Jan.–March 1952.

68 TOKYO, BRIDGESTONE GALLERY, AND OSAKA, FINE ARTS MUSEUM. J. M. W. Turner. Sept. 21–Oct. 20, and Nov. 1–30, 1963. Organized by The British Museum and The British Council. 50 exhibits.

69 TORONTO, ART GALLERY, and OTTAWA, NATIONAL GALLERY OF CANADA. An Exhibition of Paintings by J. M. W. Turner. Oct.–Dec. 1951. 70 exhibits.

70 VENICE, ESPOSIZIONE D'ARTE INTERNAZIONALE DELLA XXIV BIENNALE. Turner. 1948. Organized by The Tate Gallery and The British Council. 50 exhibits.

71 WASHINGTON, NATIONAL GALLERY OF ART, and HOUSTON, SAN FRANCISCO, CLEVELAND, KANSAS CITY and BROOKLYN. Turner Watercolors from The British Museum. Sept. 1963–May 1964. Organized by The Smithsonian Institution. 80 exhibits.

COVER: *Sun Setting over the Sea. c. 1840–5.* Oil on canvas, 36 × 48″. The Tate Gallery, London